LAST FLIGHT OUT

LAST FLIGHT OUT

True Tales of Adventure, Travel, and Fishing

Randy Wayne White

The Lyons Press
Guilford, Connecticut
An imprint of The Globe Pequot Press

The Lyons Press is an imprint of The Globe Pequot Press.

All of these stories, in shorter or edited forms, appeared in *Outside* magazine between the years 1987 and 2000, except for "Dr. Pepper," which originally appeared in *Reader's Digest*, and "Professional Camp," which originally appeared in *Men's Journal*.

10 9 8 7 6 5

Printed in the United States of America

ISBN 978-1-59228-334-7 (trade paper)

Library of Congress has cataloged an earlier hardcover edition as follows:

White, Randy Wayne.
    Last flight out : true tales of adventure, travel, and fishing / Randy Wayne White.
        p. cm.
    ISBN 1-58574-383-6
    1. White, Randy Wayne—Journeys. 2. Voyages and travels. 3. Fishing—Anecdotes.
    I. Title.

G465.W52 2002
910.4'1—dc21   2001050235

CONTENTS

INTRODUCTION

A s I write this, I am sitting in the garden plaza of a great hotel in Cartagena, Colombia. There are parrots and toucans in the palms, winter jasmine abloom, and there is the good odor of tropic wind, the Caribbean sea outside, and of a fountain drizzling water on old stone.

Prior to leaving on this trip, more than one acquaintance said to me, "Aren't you afraid to get on a plane? Isn't it a dangerous time for Americans to travel to foreign countries?"

They then proceeded to give me advice that I have received many, many times before over the last two decades, but never more anxiously than now: Paste a Canadian flag on my luggage, sew one on my travel vest. Pretend to be something I am not.

I am outwardly grateful for the concern but, inwardly, increasingly impatient with a mindset that does not question its own premise. The premise is this: Behavior motivated by fear is a more sensible approach to life than behavior motivated by a passion for living, or pride in one's own heritage.

Did I say "impatient"? Change that to "disappointed."

I read recently that board members of some kind of national teachers organization have cancelled their annual conference in my home state of Florida because travel is "just too dangerous now." This was months after the terrorist attack on 11 September, 2001.

I am not an academic, and certainly no expert on academia, but I was president of my 4-H Club and know something of the behavior of sheep. Of people who assume roles of guidance and authority—teachers, for instance—one expects, at least, sensible adult behavior if not courageous leadership. I know too many fine educators to believe this was anything but a decision made by a craven few. I take comfort in the hope that most teachers find this pitiable example of capitulation as loathsome as I.

But I am off the track. Or am I?

Nope, actually I'm right on track. This book is called *Last Flight Out* for a reason, and that reason is a Key West pal of mine, Clay Greager who, not coincidentally, owns a little store called Last Flight Out. It's located just off Duval Street, right across from Sloppy Joe's Bar, and inside he sells travel-adventure stuff, cool hats and T-shirts, and little books of poetry, too. Key West is a magnet to the world so, day after day, the whole world, in various forms and colors, troops through Clay's store. He is a sociable man, and a great storyteller, so everyone who meets the guy likes him.

There are two stories as to how Clay came up with the name Last Flight Out. One is public, a fun story to hear. The second is Clay's personal story, and it is a powerful story, indeed. Here they are, in Clay's own words:

Last Flight Out, Public Version

During the 1970s there were only two ways to either arrive or depart Key West. One was by car traveling the old U.S. 1 highway with its notorious seven-mile bridge (the bridge was extremely narrow with only inches between passing cars) and the other was

Air Sunshine, the only airline to service Key West. The first flight was at 8:00 A.M., and the last flight was at 11:00 P.M.

The airline was affectionately called "Air Sometimes" due to its inability to fly on schedule. In those days, Key West was considered one of the world's "best-kept secrets." It literally captured those who visited and the most often heard comment was "I'm not leaving until the last flight goes!" As a result, the bars (which usually closed around 10 P.M.) would announce "Last Flight Out" instead of "Last Call."

The bar at Key West airport, though, was open twenty-four hours a day and all the island's restaurant employees would just be arriving when the plane was supposed to be departing. Sometimes the plane's crew would be among the revelers and hence that was another reason the plane wasn't dependable. However this was not cause for despair, visitors just extended their stay one more day in paradise. In fact there are still people in Key West from the seventies waiting for their Last Flight Out!

Clay's Personal Story: Last Flight Out

Dear Randy,

I feel that it's necessary for me to explain the circumstances that led me across the threshold from immortality to mortality. It was a time when I learned that life itself was random, frivolous, and I was nothing special. Some may think the situation was tragic, however, I feel it was those conditions that made me realize just how precious each day is and to live my life on a daily basis, savoring each and every sunset.

1968 Landing Zone Betty
Helicopter Scout Platoon (Flying Circus)
1st Air Cavalry Division
Republic of South Vietnam

It was predawn, and I was preparing the light observation helicopter for our first mission of the day. Every day we would fly a first-light reconnaissance covering our area of operations. It was nothing more than flying around the area to see if there had been any enemy activity during the night.

The mission was generally flown without a wingman, just one OH-13 light observation helicopter, which is identical to the helicopter used in the opening scenes of the TV series *M*A*S*H*. It held only two people, the pilot and the gunner. Due to its lack of power, we wore no protective armor and only carried a limited amount of ammunition: only 400 rounds of ammo. An M-60 machine gun is capable of firing at the rate of 600 rounds a minute, so we really had to be selective.

We modified our machine guns by cutting off most of the barrel; this was because we generally stood outside on the skids and, the shorter the barrel, the easier it was to maneuver in and out of the chopper. The most dangerous part of any mission was when and if we made contact with the enemy. We were very vulnerable from underneath and behind.

A scout team had a strange relationship. The pilot had to keep the gunner between himself and the enemy. The gunner knew that because if the pilot ever became wounded, even slightly, the aircraft was doomed to crash, for there was no way for the gunner to take over the controls. The gunner became the shield and accepted that responsibility without any reservations.

So on an early morning of 1968 in the I Corp Area of South Vietnam we took off in the same manner we did every other day. The area where we were headed had had no recent enemy activity. However, there was a combat assault scheduled for that morning, so all we had to do was scout the area and let the infantry know it was safe to land. Combat assaults were run constantly as a way of keeping everybody sharp, for it was easy to become complacent even in combat.

When we got to the designated landing zone, we began hovering around looking for any hidden bunkers or signs that the enemy might be in the area. Finding nothing, I told the pilot that I was going to mark the area with a green smoke grenade to let the combat assault commander know it was okay to bring in his troops.

As I leaned out to drop the smoke grenade we immediately took a heavy barrage of enemy fire. Instantly, we were falling out of the sky.

For a microsecond, I didn't know what happened. Then my instincts took over. I knew we were badly hit and about to crash. Being only twenty feet or so off the ground, there was nothing we could do. It's amazing how fast a person can react. My reflexes just acted on their own. I sat back in the seat, slapped and locked in my harness, pulled the M-60 unto my lap and held my head back as far as I could. I knew the rotor blades have a bad habit of dipping down and chopping off whatever gets in their way.

Once we hit, I unlocked my harness, pushed the machine gun out in front of me. I knew that when I ran around the front of the chopper the ammo belt would tear off, and I'd at least have some ammo with me. I didn't even have time to lean down and scoop up the loose belt of ammo that lay at my feet.

The pilot and I ran a few feet and tried to hide in a slight depression in the ground. In those first few seconds, lying there on the ground, I'd never been so afraid in my life. This couldn't be happening, I thought. Then the real fear set in.

When we went down, the helicopters carrying the infantry troops overhead saw us hit the ground and all hell breaking loose. They'd radioed back that we were down and probably line 1's. Line 1's was the code for dead, Line 2's were for wounded. All they saw were the two of us lying flat down on the ground and not moving.

So there we were, both laying facedown in the dirt unable to even lift our heads to see what was going on. All I knew was the enemy had us and we couldn't escape. The enemy also knew they could use us for bait. They were so close! I couldn't fire back, first of all I didn't have enough ammo but most of all I was not about to lift my head up to fire. We lay there for a long time not even daring to turn over and look up. We were really close to the enemy, so it was not possible for the arriving cobra gun ships to even fire their rockets for fear of hitting us. Thank God there was a question as to whether we were dead or alive.

When it first happened, I started to pray to God, *Please let me live*. However, that changed as time went by. I went through several transitions. At first, I prayed for my life. Then I prayed not to be taken prisoner. Then I prayed that I would be shot and killed but not wounded. There came a time when I feared the waves of fear that engulfed me more than I feared dying.

I was lying on my machine gun with the barrel under my chin. I kept saying to myself, if I felt anyone grab me I would pull the trigger. Time went on eternally and all I can remember is I wanted to die and get this over with. There was nothing left inside. I just wanted it to end. The ironic thing looking back is that I never considered pulling the trigger unless I was about to be captured. My mind just didn't have that option. Also, contrary to what I heard in the past, I never had a thought about family or anything else except the situation I was in.

After several hours, the artillery began to bracket the area, rounds moving in closer and closer. They were very accurate and we just lay there listening to the incoming rounds. It became evident we were being used as bait and then we realized that if the enemy decided to break off, they would just run right over and kill us. All I thought about was make it fast. I had seen others die and knew it could be over in a second or two. A headshot was what I prayed for.

Sometime late in the afternoon, the artillery really began to land their rounds in our general area. Closer and closer they came. Who was going to be the winner was not the question, now we were worried they would overshoot the enemy and land on us. You could hear the rounds coming in from far away and then the screeching as they got close and the wham of the explosion.

After several hours it got quiet and stayed quiet. We still didn't lift up our heads. Then we heard the Huey, that *wop-wop* of the blades breaking through the air as it came hovering down over us.

Both the pilot and I just reached up and grabbed the skids. We hung on and the Huey moved a short distance away and the door gunners pulled both of us inside. I was just sitting there next to the crew chief looking out and wondering why people think life is so precious. There are no guarantees and no one is special. I should have been killed, I prayed to die, and yet here I was being taken back to my landing zone.

There was a combat photographer on board who had been sent out to cover the rescue. After a while he reached over and tapped me on the shoulder. I looked over at him and he said, "Damn, that was exciting." I didn't answer. Years later I moved to Key West and created a store called **LAST FLIGHT OUT**.

* * *

Recently, Clay repeated what he's told me before: The LFO story doesn't exclusively apply to Key West or Vietnam. It doesn't even have to deal with a location. We all have a Last Flight Out within us. As he puts it, "It's that wistful thinking of who you'd like to be. Where you'd like to be . . . and with whom you'd like to be.

"It's that ultimate escape in your mind. That last thought right before you fall asleep. Change careers, change locations, find a partner. Don't say: 'I can't!' Believe in yourself! Step out on that ten-meter diving board, close your eyes and lean forward, trust there is water in the pool. *Stop* going back down the ladder. Believe that just for today, the sun rises only for you. . . ."

Meet someone like Clay, and it's difficult not to be disappointed by fellow countrymen who think that behavior motivated by fear is a more sensible approach to life than behavior motivated by a passion for living or pride in one's own heritage.

I believe there are, fortunately, far more Clay Greagers in this country than the kind of sheep who live so fitfully, so shallowly, that they can't muster the courage for a trip to Orlando.

I am not the bravest of souls. I'd run a mile to avoid a fight— farther, if my old catcher's knees could stand it. The idea of taking risks just for the adrenaline thrill gives me the willies. However, I have traveled enough, done enough, seen enough to know that a passive, sedentary life is predacious as slow cancer. To live with one's fingers upon one's pulse is not living. Furthermore, to allow oneself to be bullied by thugs is to be a deserter to the obligations of our own heritage.

So grab a boat or train or plane and go. We've all got your own personal Last Flight Out waiting. As for me, I'm having a great time in Colombia. Wish you were here.

—Randy Wayne White
Hotel Santa Clara
Cartagena de Indes, Colombia
November 2001
RWWHITE.COM

A SECOND INTRODUCTION: AN OPEN LETTER TO HE WHO HIDES BEHIND THE CASKET OF INNOCENTS

On Tuesday morning, September 11, 2001, you delivered onto our nation yet another public invitation, and then, characteristically, fled into the shadows. Because your invitation was written on the flesh of innocents, and with the blood of our heroes, it demands a response.

A short time ago, most of us would have declined out of indifference, out of ignorance. We were an insulated people, secure in the triumphs of our forefathers.

Not today. Not ever again. In the last few hours, we have aged a generation. Our indifference lies beneath rubble in a great city, so your invitation—as much as we loath your methods—is now most welcome. We welcome it because you have forced us to understand that the event which you press upon us is inevitable and unavoidable. You have invited us to a Day of Reckoning. We accept. That Day of Reckoning will soon come.

If our response seems unexpectedly strong, it may be because we were never the people you thought us to be. You have said publicly that you believe Americans to be weak, spoiled by our own wealth. You have said that we lack courage, resolve, and morality. You have said that we are a mongrel nation, a nation divided by racial hatred and class warfare.

Perhaps it would be good to explain to you who we really are, and so thereby remind ourselves exactly what our heritage now demands of us.

We are the sons and daughters of every race, all religions, the world's yearning masses, joined between two oceans and by a passion for self-determination and freedom. Don't assume, because we use hyphens as identifiers, that a hyphen can divide us. A hyphen also connects. Our own history proves, again and again, that in times of national emergency, we are all defined by one word, not two: American.

In us runs the blood of revolutionaries and explorers, of farmers, immigrants and Algonquin statesmen, of train barons and train robbers, and of individuals who, though chained to slave ships, refused to bow down as slaves. We are people who risked the gallows to create a sanctuary on Earth that, for the first time in mankind's history, guaranteed religious freedom to all, as well as life, liberty, and the pursuit of happiness. A mongrel nation? Absolutely. You may have forgotten the first time you spoke those words. It was in Berlin, 1939.

We forgot, too, for a time. Thanks for reminding us.

Do we lack courage, resolve, and morality? You will soon curse the day that you doubted. We are the 50,000 who took our strong convictions to earth at Gettysburg. We are the thousands of white crosses that rest where poppies grow at Flanders Field in Belgium. We are Doolittle's Raiders and Patton's blood and guts. We are the 101st Airborne Screaming Eagles who parachuted into Normandy—my own father among them—and we are the body of a lone Army Ranger that your followers dragged naked through the streets of Somalia.

We are the 7th Cavalry who perished at Little Big Horn. We are Apache warriors who refused to run, and so stood awaiting death while chanting a powerful refrain: "Your bullets stand no chance against our prayers!"

To understand us? Read Thoreau and Emerson, Martin Luther King and the speeches of Tecumseh. We are not an easy people. We love a winner and despise a coward. Courage is our national cornerstone, and we are at our best when we demonstrate courage as individuals. Our reverence for self-reliance has never been equaled, nor will it ever be. We are Teddy Roosevelt charging up San Juan Hill on horseback and exploring rain-forest rivers by canoe. We are Lou Gehrig saying a fearless farewell. We are Rosa Parks, with tired feet, refusing to move to the back of the bus. We are John Wayne, standing tall, fighting cancer, and we are a great American Muslim named Muhammad Ali, devoted to his beliefs of right and wrong.

Tough? Send a boxing team to the Olympics. Better yet, send your strongest to Manhattan. We have some heroic fire fighters there who'd purely love to meet your best. Don't bother bringing gloves.

No. You cannot possibly know who we are, what we are, or you would not have risked the delivery of your cowardly message.

The difficult question for us as Americans, though, is not will we triumph, but how? Our quandary is this: In any conflict, the boundaries of acceptable behavior are defined by the party that cares least about morality.

You have defined the boundaries, and there are none. The lives of the innocent, of women, children, and good men, are meaningless. You hide weapon factories beneath day-care centers. You hide collectively behind the caskets of innocents. You have no morality, no character or conscience, while we Americans are blessed—and burdened—by all three.

No matter. We will find a way. Americans always have. As Americans, we always will. Your invitation to us was written in the blood of our own heroes, so we have no choice but to accept. Your Day of Reckoning is near. If there is any justice, a century from now, history will still hear the weeping of your widows. The world will agree that those of us who died that terrible Tuesday did not die in vain.

Your cowardice cannot stand in the face of our resolve. Your Evil has no chance against our prayers.

—Randy Wayne White
Pine Island, Florida

LAST FLIGHT OUT

CAT ISLAND

Before explaining how I became the confidant of practitioners of Obeah, or voodoo, and before describing how my friend Mallow demonstrated his own cunning and cowardice by tricking me into camping alone at the site of more than one devilish Black Mass, I must first explain why I traveled to Cat Island in the Bahamas if you are to believe what happened or why it happened, and if you are to understand why Mallow and his spineless ilk should never again draw another easy Christian breath in my presence.

It was Mallow who, a month earlier, had telephoned with what sounded like just another drunken Caribbean tale but, in fact, turned out to be mostly true. A Bahamian he knew had found what Mallow called a treasure chest in the ruins of a Cat Island plantation house. Since the plantation house dated back to the 1700s, and since a locksmith had recently judged the chest to be between three hundred and four hundred years old, the contents were of interest.

"The trouble is," Mallow said, "Tony won't open the chest." (He was talking about Tony Armbrister, whose family came to the island in 1780.) "The locksmith said that he would have to destroy it to open it. And since the box belonged to Tony's ancestors [Sir William Edward Armbrister], Tony says he'd rather have the box than what's inside it. Not even his wife can talk him into opening the thing."

It was Mallow's belief that I, with the promise of publicity, might be able to change Tony's mind. I was dubious, but it would be interesting to see this old iron box, so I decided to go to Cat Island—a decision not made quickly, for I am not a fan of the Bahamas. But Cat Island, located 142 miles southeast of Nassau, wasn't like other islands in the Bahamas I have visited, which is to say that I loved it because it is exactly what I wanted a tropical island to be: it is remote and wind tattered with empty beaches edged by coconut palms, plus its citizenry has not been transformed into predators and wastrels by a jetstream of tourism. On Cat Island (not to be confused with Cat Key, a fishing resort near Bimini) the island's two thousand inhabitants still fish and work their gardens, growing bananas, yams, papayas, and peas, just as islanders have for the last two hundred years.

Because better-known islands in the Bahamas are what they are, it is easier to describe Cat Island by noting what it is not and what it does not have. Cat Island has no Club Meds, no Jet Ski concessions, no disco drunk factories, no cold-weather sex trade, no obnoxious rental scooters, no paved roads, and no crime to speak of. For some happy reason, the resort pirates had overlooked this place, although the island isn't small. It is forty-six miles long and shaped like an old crone's boot: mostly narrow as rattan except for its deltaic southern base. There are a couple of airstrips (Bahamas Air flies in four times a week), but no jetports, and there are no cities, only a scattering of lime-and-wattle settlements with names that echo the lassitude of enduring in a place dominated by rock, thorn, wind, and sea.

Unlike most islands, Cat Island still retains the integrity of its own isolation. That's what I liked most about it. And the Armbrister stronghold, Fernandez Bay Village (one of the few places to stay on Cat Island), meshed prettily with the island and its history. Fernandez Bay, a rind of white beach and clear-water harbor, is where, nearly thirty years ago, the family's matron, Frances Armbrister (called Mrs. A. by everyone on the island), and son Tony decided to build a few rental cottages on land granted to their loyalist family during the American Revolution. The results are a tropical reverie. The villas are built of stone and wood with high ceilings and lofts that open out onto the sea. The main house serves three excellent meals a day (Tony, a pilot, flies in supplies—and guests—from Fort Lauderdale), and there is a beach bar that operates on the honor system. If you want a cold bottle of beer, you simply wipe the ice off it and sign your name on the clipboard.

So I was glad I came to Cat Island, metal chest or no metal chest. Each morning, I would zombie walk from bed straight into the sea and swim the quarter mile out to the reef and back. Then I'd read for a while, or go for a bike ride with my eleven-year-old son, Rogan. Rogan was wild about the place, too. (As Tony's wife, Pam, told me, "The wonderful thing about Cat Island is that you can let your children run free. It's safe here.") In the afternoon, we'd jog down the beach or pedal down to Smith's Bay and fly cast to the resident bonefish. In the evening, we lingered over meals on the beach terrace, listening to Mrs. A. tell stories. (She, a Hollywood starlet, and her husband, producer of the radio show *The Shadow*, returned to the island in 1938.)

In other words, we enjoyed a sort of idyllic island existence.

But there was a treasure chest, just like Mallow said. Tony kept it in the main house by the fireplace. My first day, he let me wrestle with it—the thing was built of slab iron, ancient in appearance, and must have weighed two hundred pounds. "My mother and some friends dug it out of the ruins of one of the old stone houses," Tony told me, giving the kind of shrug that illustrates finality. "I could use a blowtorch to get into it, but think of how long it's been in my family. Even if it has gold doubloons in it, it's more valuable to me the way it is." Then he added, "Mallow knows that. I'm surprised he brought you down here on a wild goose chase."

I wasn't surprised. Mallow is shifty by nature and trouble by design. He has spent his life involved with one kind of Caribbean intrigue or another, and his enthusiasm, though refreshing, too often masks schemes that are always convoluted and sometimes just plain dangerous. Early in our stay, he showed his stripe by stealing our lunches, then short-sheeting our beds. His practical jokes were incessant; ultimately, shaving cream was involved. Worse, he began to exert influence on my own son. Too soon, I was running alone and fishing alone while Rogan, by choice, remained in the thatched shade of the cabana bar under Mallow's delinquent guidance. I found this disconcerting, for my fatherly definition of adventure has never included ogling island women through a rum haze. Even more troubling was Mallow's intent. Why had he lured us to this tropical paradise? What hellish juvenile prank did his elaborate ruse mask? Fearing a blindside attack, I remained on full alert. Which is why I was wary when Mallow began pestering: "Now that you've gotten this treasure chest thing out of your system, we ought to get away from Fernandez Bay. You know, do something *exciting*."

One night after dinner, Mallow goaded Mrs. A. into telling stories about Obeah, the island's underground religion. It was a favorite topic of hers and, frankly, of mine because, having traveled widely throughout the Caribbean, I am interested in voodoo, Santeria, and their kindred. So Mrs. A. told us about her friend Lavida's daughter, Judy, who became the target of "a salt Obeah" (*assault* Obeah, I would learn later), the effect of which was nearly fatal.

"At night," Mrs. A. said, "hands came down out of the darkness and choked her—that's the way Judy described it. Judy was an intelligent, educated woman, but she was terrified. The fact that the practice of Obeah has been outlawed by the Bahamian government makes it no less powerful."

As usual, we were on the beach in torchlight where the eighty-five-year-old Mrs. A. held court: a regal lady whose flowing white dress added a formal quality while demonstrating that she had long ago made peace with exigencies of island living. Beside her were Tony, who looks more like a young Ivy League professor than an island bush pilot, and Pam, a woman of great beauty, wearing a blue sarong and, in her hair, a coral red hibiscus blossom. Also in attendance were Steve, a hulking artist (whom I privately believed to be a little mad and potentially dangerous), and, of course, Mallow. The beach was deserted; we sat in a cluster, leaning to hear Mrs. A.'s soft, sure voice.

"Judy was dying," she said. "We tried medical doctors, but they couldn't help. Finally, in desperation, Lavida took Judy to a Haitian healer who lived in Nassau. A Houngan—'vitch doctor' we might call him here. The Houngan took one look at Judy and said that she had been hexed. They stared into a crystal ball, and Lavida saw the people who had placed the Obeah on Judy—the jealous parents of a girl who wanted Judy's job. The father had already given Judy two doses of something, the vitch doctor said. The third and final dose would be fatal. But the vitch doctor called upon Judy's dead grandfather to intercede and protect her. A week or so later, the man was riding horseback to Lavida's house when the ghost of the grandfather rose up out of the road. The horse spooked and the man was badly injured. The Obeah was broken. Now Judy is a happy, healthy woman and has children." Mrs. A. smiled, pleased with her own story. "After over half a century on this island, I've learned that Obeah is serious business."

It was a compelling tale; Mrs. A. had a huge repertory of such stories, for her own history, the history of Cat Island, and the practice of Obeah were inexorably intertwined. It still thrived on the island, she said, which led to a discussion of the present. Mallow said he had heard that an abandoned hermitage had become the midnight meeting place for what he called "those voodoo folks," though he meant practitioners of vaudun, the ancient dark arts. He was talking about a stone hermitage that sat atop Mount Alvernia (at 206 feet, the highest peak in all the Bahamas) and was built by Friar Jerome Hawes, a recluse who lived in a cave while he constructed the retreat as penance, stone by slow stone. I had seen the place from a distance, and it looked less like a monastery than a medieval castle, with its parapets, domed roofs, and bell tower; it was an eerie reminder of the Dark Ages on a hill that shimmered with heat.

"It'd be interesting to camp there," Mallow said, indicating the four of us—himself, me, Rogan, and the mad artist. "We might see some ghosts" (he meant Wangas and Duppies), "or hear some of their secret spells" (he meant Langay, a sacred language of African origin). Then Mallow eyed me pointedly. "You're not afraid, are you? You're not superstitious?"

I play baseball, fish, and often fly in small planes. Of course I'm superstitious. But this adolescent challenge was made in the presence of my son. To back down was to imply cowardice and, worse, might strengthen Mallow's churlish influence on an impressionable boy. So I replied, "I'd love to camp at the hermitage. In fact, it's the sort of thing I'd normally do alone. But if you guys want to go, I'll look after you as best I can." Which, I felt, put Mallow right in his place.

We were two days away from the full moon, a Wednesday, and we agreed it would be the ideal night. That decided, we put the topic aside and continued with our normal island routine—at least, Mallow and the mad artist did, but I only pretended to. In truth, I busied myself doing research on the island's Obeah community. Would the true believers be offended if we camped at the hermitage? That was a consideration. Pitching a tent, uninvited, on the floor of a Carolina Baptist church invited a well-deserved thrashing, and our impiety might summon the Cat Island equivalent. With the help of Tony and Mrs. A., I secured the name of a local man, Victor Smith, whom they said might be knowledgeable. "Victor's grandfather was said to be a very important Obeah man," Mrs. A. told me, before warning, "but don't be surprised if Victor won't talk about it. It's all secret, you know."

I found Victor Smith at the home he had built himself, a comfortable CBS house, spotlessly maintained. He offered me beer, and I sat at the kitchen table, listening as this articulate man confirmed that his late grandfather had, indeed, been a powerful man on the island. "He was known as Thunder," Victor explained, "but that was in back times, a long time ago." Which I took as polite evasion, not that I blamed him. We spent the next half hour making general conversation, which is how we discovered, to our mutual surprise, that we were both members of a secret fraternal organization—a fraternity that has nothing to do with college. Instantly, we were confidants, and Smith promised to introduce me to the island Houngan who, because he was a fellow brother, would tell me whatever I wanted to know. "But you won't be allowed to publish all that you hear," Smith said. Then he reminded me, "Don't forget, we're both bound by the same oath, man!"

The Houngan (I can't use his name) received us warmly in a room that housed shelves of bottles, vials, and rows of candles. On a wooden table was an open Bible, one page crossed out with black electrical tape. When he noticed me staring, the Houngan asked, "What your favorite psalm be?"

It is not a question that one often hears, but I had a ready reply: the Ninety-first Psalm. In my line of work, the Scripture regarding pestilence, arrows, and thousands dropping like flies is eerily applicable.

"I got a better one for you, brother," the Houngan said. "Lot stronger than that!" He spent the next minutes teaching me what he called "the special psalms" before he began to go into great detail, describing the power of an assault Obeah, and the ingredients and ceremony necessary to empower it. There were other spells: love Obeahs and death Obeahs and banishment Obeahs. ("The banishment Obeah of interest? I tell you just how we do it. But first I got to know the person's name!")

I learned that there are three main components in the craft: physical, biblical, and numerical, and that the lost books of Moses were sometimes employed, as were coarse salt, spirits of turpentine, blue stones from Haiti, Chipman paper, fire, and blood. All important ceremonies were held at midnight or 6 A.M., often in cemeteries. To illustrate the power of a death Obeah, the Houngan recounted a recent event: a local man, Ali Russell, was murdered in Nassau. Russell's father contacted the Houngan, asking for revenge. At midnight, the Houngan visited Ali's corpse at the mortuary and, after performing a complex ceremony, placed a raw egg in Ali's hand. Within a week, two of the murderers were beheaded in a motorcycle crash, and two others were killed in a car crash. Again at midnight, the Houngan exhumed Ali's body and found that the fresh egg was now broken. "That one stinking thing!" the Houngan told me. "The egg, I mean. Plus, that Ali, he weren't in too good shape, neither. But it proved they all dead; all the conspirators!"

Before leaving, I told the Houngan that I was planning to camp the night at the abandoned hermitage. "Should be all right," he said, "but don't tell nobody you're doing it. Keep it private, man. Real personal." He offered to anoint me with some protective oil.

"I buy it from a Haitian lady, lives in Nassau. Miz Nola. Two hundred fifty dollars a vial!"

I accepted the oil. The Houngan refused my offer of payment.

On Wednesday, the night of the full moon, Mallow backed out. As an excuse for his shameless crawfishing, he used mosquitoes, spiders, all kinds of weak reasons. The mad artist followed suit, and then Rogan said, "I'll go if you really want me to, but I'd rather stay here. They're having cake for dessert."

So I headed out alone. To get to the hermitage, you drive several miles of washboard road, then turn east through the stone entranceway of a plantation ruin. After that tight squeeze, it's another quarter mile down a carriage lane, then you climb Mount Alvernia on steps chiseled out by Father Hawes. When I got to the top, I explored the hermitage, hunching my way through the tiny chapel, the vestry, and the canoe-size sleeping chamber (the man must have been a dwarf), then I sat outside atop the crevice where Hawes lies interred.

Behind, the moon was rising; before me, the sun was setting, and Cat Island, alone on a bronze sea, floated in the balance. Below, the first frail lights of the twilight villages glittered while everything else receded into smoky shadow: the unpopulated land regions of an island that, by benefit of isolation, retained the extract of its own history—a rare thing in the Bahamas.

Spells were still cast here, and those spells struck at the marrow. Unopened treasure chests seemed drab in comparison.

I didn't camp; hadn't planned to. I just wanted to watch the moon rise and listen to island sounds. But I did stay until nearly midnight. I was wearing the protective oil, yet why push my luck? When I returned to Fernandez Bay, the Armbristers, the mad artist, Mallow, and Rogan were all sitting outside, roaring with laughter. They seemed loony with moonlight.

"You thought I was going to sneak up there and scare you!" Mallow called out.

That was the joke. I was to have stayed at the hermitage, anticipating an attack, while he lay around in comfort, sipping rum. Not that it came as a surprise. Rogan had warned me that morning before asking, "You think Mallow will ever act his age?"

Now sitting at the table, my young son shook his head and winked at me—confirmation of our private alliance.

Then I began laughing—but for a reason none of them knew. The name I had given the Houngan was Mallow's.

ABOVE SUSPICION

Meeting hellish deadlines when in the field is tough enough without attempting to compose while strapped into a Volkswagen-size Cessna 182, flying at 7,500 feet across the border of Baja California en route to undetermined destinations with my friend G. H. "This time," he said from the left seat, "when the military tries to arrest me, I want you to snap a picture. Last year they detained me thirty-two times, and I don't have a single photograph to prove it. You know—something I can frame for my office wall. They're camera shy and trigger-happy. It's a dicey combination, so try not to be obvious about it."

In terms of dicey combinations, the trip ahead of us seemed daunting enough: ten days in an overloaded single-engine two-seater, exploring the deserts and mountains and desolate coasts of the Baja peninsula. As a lifelong tight-sphincter flier, I found the prospect of dozens of bush landings and takeoffs sufficiently frightening without adding the potential for gunplay. "Photograph the *federales*?" I asked. "Why don't I save us all some time and just open the door and jump?"

Like most pilots who are focused on flying, G. H. was numb to hyperbole. "Don't even think about it," he said. "We're tail-heavy as it is. Without your weight, we'll rear up like a horse when I try to land."

G. H. is Galen Hanselman of Hailey, Idaho, a bush pilot who looks the part, with his leather flight jacket, his beard, and his Indiana Jones fedora. But he's also the publisher and author of a valuable little book called *Fly Idaho!* The book was originally intended for working bush pilots, but because planes go where cars can't, it's proved to be a popular guide for anyone interested in the Idaho backcountry. G. H. was now working on a kind of sequel, *Air Baja!* "Baja is a terrible place to drive," he said, "but it's perfect for small planes." Like his previous book, *Air Baja!* would be a no-nonsense, ring-bound air traveler's guide and would contain precise aeronautical data as well as low-altitude photos of landing approaches.

I'd joined G. H. on the trip for a couple of reasons. One was that he'd promised me that there's a quantum difference between traveling by plane and exploring by plane—a distinction few of us get the chance to experience.

The second reason I was sitting sweaty palmed in that cramped cockpit was that he needed someone to help him photograph and measure some of the hundred dirt airstrips that would be featured in his new book. And as I'd already been warned, he was unable to obtain a permit to take commercial photographs, so all photos would have to be made surreptitiously—a task that had seemed mildly adventurous at first but now, with the news of G. H.'s many detainments, seemed decidedly unsound.

G. H., who is in his late forties, looks and acts more like a kindly physics professor than a bandit. So why would anyone give him a hard time? "Some of the landing strips were built by drug runners," he explained. "And since I do a lot of quick landings and takeoffs and scouting around, I fit a certain profile. So remember: when they surround the plane and raise their weapons, just stay calm."

Coming through his little plane's scratchy communications system, G. H.'s voice had a rock-solid, Right Stuff quality that should have been reassuring but wasn't. Below us was a valley bordered by small, peach-colored mountains. From horizon to horizon, earth tones were as subtly stratified as a Hopi sand painting, and the only indications of life were vultures circling beneath us, their shadows sailing across the hardpan.

Then the hills tilted precariously as G. H. banked, and I had to fight the nauseating sensation that I might tumble out the door. The little plane rattled and bucked as the altimeter swept counterclockwise. The earth grew larger and swelled with detail through the front window. G. H. leveled her off, and we sped across the mottled desert at a mere hundred feet. We passed over an expanding salt flat funneled like a river delta, then suddenly shot out over the Gulf of California, shimmering in the sunlight.

For fifty miles, we flew along the beach, where there were only wading birds and gulls and big fish flushing from the shallows: no boats, no houses, no man-spore of any kind.

In the last year, G. H. has made ten research trips to Baja, and he has a solid work routine. He establishes a base camp, unloads gear to lighten his plane, and then takes off again to scout out interesting places and usable airstrips. When he finds an unfamiliar strip, he lands and measures its length and width with a calibrated measuring wheel. Then he hikes off and asks people the kinds of questions travelers ask: what's the local history? Are there good spots to camp and fish and go nosing around? His readers, he says, want more than just information on where to park their planes.

How many pilots would be willing to pay forty dollars for such a book? I asked him. "There are close to a million of us in the United States," he replied. "People who travel in private aircraft make up one of the quietest subcultures around. They're self-reliant and good at what they do, so you don't hear much about them. Not that they all buy my books—I sold about five thousand copies of *Fly Idaho!* But I don't do the books because I expect to make a lot of money. I do it because I love the research. It gives me an excuse to fly and explore—my two favorite things to do."

We'd already done a good bit of exploring. The day before, we'd made a base camp near the Bay of San Luis Gonzaga at a funky little settlement of beach shacks called Alfonsina's. We'd had to wait for the falling tide to expose the mud landing strip before we could wheel the Cessna up behind our room. Soon after our arrival, a Humvee loaded with soldiers charged up the strip after us and demanded our papers. But the soldiers were cheerful and polite. They kept their weapons slung and didn't even bother to search the plane. The officer in charge gracefully accepted G. H.'s gift, a twenty-five-pound sack of beans.

"Maybe they've relaxed their attitude toward private aircraft," G. H. said, pleased not only by the reception but also by the chance to part with all those heavy beans. Or maybe it was just that the kicked-back attitude of Alfonsina's was contagious. A dozen or so men had just rolled in from Tijuana, and they hadn't even knocked the dust off their clothes before they invited us to the bachelor party they had planned for that evening.

"Do you know those guys?" I asked.

"Never seen them before in my life," G. H. said.

We sat on the beach eating roasted clams, drinking Pacifico Clara beer, and watching a full moon emerge from a windy sea. Even G. H., who doesn't drink alcohol while on flying trips, was unable to decipher who the prospective groom was, but it didn't much matter to us and seemed to matter less to them. We were part of their group, and they made sure that we were included in every toast and every joke.

"Go ahead—drink up and have fun," G. H. said before heading off to bed. "I'm not flying tomorrow."

About midnight, someone produced a trunkload of musical instruments, and I spent the next couple of hours playing maracas and bongos to songs I'd never heard before. Soon I was getting teary-eyed right along with my *compañeros* at every sad song.

The next morning—it couldn't have been much after sunrise—I awoke to G. H. pounding at my cabana door. "The plane's all set," he said. "You ready to go?" I blinked my way around the room— whitewashed walls, raw cement floor, bare lightbulb hanging from the ceiling, seatless commode coated with sand.

Thank God, I was still in Baja.

I sat up and said, "You told me you weren't flying today."

"I'm not flying today," G. H. replied, already turning toward the little gray-and-white Cessna parked just outside. "I'm taking pictures while *you* fly."

Eight hundred miles long and only sixty miles wide, Baja California is a fragile land break immersed in the open sea. Isolated by geography and its own poor road system, the peninsula is intimately connected with wind and stars and the cataclysms of geology. When the Transpeninsular Highway linked Tijuana to Cabo San Lucas in 1973, cynics predicted that Baja would be overrun with tourists. While that's exactly what's happened to Cabo, that thin ribbon of asphalt otherwise has done little to destroy the peninsula's pristine wildness.

Over the next few days, while steadily working our way south, I spent longer and longer stints at the controls, stints that at first left me white-knuckled and breathless. Gradually, though, all the flaps and flight gauges that had been a blur to me began to assume individual consequence, and I began to master the niceties of trim. G. H.'s prediction was on the money—I was coming to enjoy exploring by plane. Often, when crossing the mountains that run down the spine of Baja, we flew at an altitude that allowed us to see both the Pacific Ocean and the Gulf of California. The peninsula between—wrinkled, jagged—stretched beneath us like some immense topo map.

The strangest place we visited was an island in the gulf, San Marcos, where there is an industrial village that houses employees of a large gypsum mining company. Landing on San Marcos was like landing on the bright side of the moon. On one of the hillsides sat a bone white church, and to the left of the airstrip was a baseball stadium complete with bleachers and a wooden outfield wall that proclaimed HOME OF THE SAN MARCOS STARS in bright orange paint. We saw men riding in mining cars, men dwarfed by rock-grinding equipment. The island was controlled by the scream of a steam whistle. Each time we heard it, there was a flurry of human movement in the far quarries. No one ever came to inquire why we were walking up and down their airstrip, pushing a measuring wheel.

Another odd place was the Diamond Eden Hotel, near the town of Loreto. It was originally built as a golf resort, but poor returns inspired its transformation into a 183-room nudist colony, which now boasts the largest and "hottest" in-the-buff Jacuzzi in all of Mexico. "If we try to take pictures here," G. H. told me as we flew low over the place, "we might have our first real trouble with the military."

At first, G. H. seemed grateful that the Mexican military was being so nice to us. But slowly his gratitude turned to disappointment, as more and more soldiers kept meeting us with grins. "What the hell's happened?" he asked me one afternoon after yet another pleasant encounter. "Truth is, it takes some of the adventure out of things."

If so, then the adventure was suddenly put back into the equation upon landing at the Pacific Coast town of San Carlos, a popular tourist destination during the winter whale-watching season. As we taxied to a stop, we found ourselves surrounded by Mexican marines, dressed in blue field uniforms and boonie hats and carrying Heckler & Koch G-3 automatic weapons. These guys weren't smiling. Indeed, they appeared irritated and eager for action. "Pin on your ID tag!" G. H. whispered before he climbed out of the plane—by which he meant the officious laminated identification cards he'd had made for us because, he said, soldiers are impressed by such things.

I clipped my tag to my pocket and stepped out onto the tarmac. The biggest marine—a sergeant with bulldog shoulders and a state cop attitude—started interrogating us. Why had we landed in San Carlos? Where else had we landed this morning? When G. H. told him about the several isolated strips we had visited, I saw the sergeant raise his eyebrows in interest. In that case, he said, he wanted to see our passports immediately and would have to inspect our plane.

I returned to the Cessna and dug through my backpack until I found my passport. It wasn't until I turned around that I realized one of the marines had followed me and was standing there with his rifle up and ready. I offered my passport as if it were a soiled tissue.

For twenty minutes, we answered questions and signed forms that I did not understand. It wasn't until we were back in the plane again and taxiing that I realized, for the first time in my life, I actually looked forward to the prospect of being aloft, alone and unencumbered by bureaucrats or mountains or sea barriers. I yearned for the sky's vantage point, for the illusion of omniscience that is, illusion or not, a kind of freedom.

G. H. drew back on the yoke, and the Cessna lifted off the ground. Soon the village of San Carlos was but a speck in the distance, and the desert hills and jade water of Baja were once again wide and easy and wild beneath us.

THE MAN WITH THE IRON CAST

In decades to come, when the Vail Ironman Fly-fishing Championship of the World has acquired the respect it deserves, when networks are battling over rights to exclusive coverage, when shoe companies and nutrition behemoths are baiting participants with cold cash and long-term endorsement contracts, it is likely—very likely—that Glenn Lokay, the event's founder, will look back on the list of inaugural contestants and pause long enough to curse my name.

If the man can remember my name. Nothing against Lokay, but the degenerate lifestyle of western fly-fishing guides is well documented. Brain cells are the first casualties of their loathsome excesses. Put these men and women in chest waders and their passion for respectable, productive lives dissolves as quickly as their regard for personal hygiene. Place them in a bar or in the gutter of any far-flung mountain town—ditto. All they talk about, all they care about, is moving water and wild trout. Paint sniffers are more engaging dinner companions.

Which is why I was so surprised when, last fall, Lokay telephoned to invite me to his Ironman of Fly-fishing. "The first annual," he called it—a wistful name that not only implied there would be a second but also credited Lokay with foresight and organizational skills not often associated with people who have built their lives around animals that spawn.

"I've invited all the top Colorado guides west of the Divide," Lokay told me. "But we'd also like to get some saltwater fly fishermen involved. A real world championship, see? Naturally, your name is at the top of my list."

As a western guide, Lokay is atypical only in that he owns his own tackle shop, Gore Creek Fly Fisherman, in Vail, and he is often emboldened by this patina of respectability. Even so, it was uncharacteristic of him to resort to such noxious flattery.

"Let me guess," I countered. "It's October and Vail has more empty rooms than the Bates Motel. Now you've contrived some absurd competition to rally your business." "I'm going to ignore that," Lokay responded. "This is a legitimate event. Too many people view fly fishing as a snob sport. I don't blame them. The Ironman is a reply from those of us who still do it for fun. We've only had a week to plan it. I don't know how many will show up, but it's going to be great. Next year people will be begging to compete."

I listened as Lokay described the events: distance casting. Fly casting one hole of golf. Blindfolded knot tying. Accuracy casting. A one-fly fish-off. An upriver distance run, through Vail, dressed only in underwear. "You had to be drunk when you thought this thing up," I said.

"Well, sure . . . *legally*." Then Lokay added, "This'll be a real test of your abilities. A chance to show the river guides just how good you saltwater casters really are." More flattery, and utterly transparent. Lokay, aware that I know nothing about trout fishing, apparently saw this as an opportunity to debase saltwater fly fishermen everywhere for the benefit of those fops and mystical brie eaters who dominate the sport's western regions.

I decided to play along. "You really think I have a shot at winning?" I asked.

"Not even if God drops everything else just to help," Lokay answered. "The costume competition is your best hope. But remember, this is Vail, and we have standards. Buy underwear."

Driving west from Denver for the first time in many years, I noticed far fewer pickup trucks racked with Winchesters and Remingtons but a great increase in the number of Range Rovers, Land Cruisers, and Beemers rack-rigged for kayaks, mountain bikes, and fly rods. I read the clever bumper stickers as they flew past me on I-70: VISUALIZE WORLD PEACE and KEEP YOUR FLY DRY. A state once controlled by stockmen, Colorado has become an alternative-lifestyle magnet for modem cowboys, many of them immigrant Californians who are stock smart but have never branded a stray in their lives. Not that they, the Radofornians, dominate the state's spirit. Colorado is too big, too varied for that. As I drove toward the Gore Mountains, I was confident that transcendent New Agers down in Boulder were hara-deep in aromatherapy, that the Denver Think Tank Center was crackling with fresh ways to become the financial titan of the New West, while in borderline roustabout towns such as Glenwood Springs and Rangely, certain Old West types were cleaning their varmint rifles, filled with the hope and anticipation that some yupster's poodle would trespass within hollow-point range. . . .

Yes, I was mustering a competitive cynicism. Still smarting from Lokay's words ("if God drops everything else"), I was an angry flatlander priming myself for the Ironman Fly-fishing Championship of the World. I carried this foul disposition right into Vail, a Swiss Deco community where the image of jet-set wealth is underscored by local cops, who drive Audi patrol cars. Ironically, it was Vail, surprising Vail, that softened my mood. It was October in the Rockies, and winter was working its way down the mountains.

Altitude could be gauged by faint demarcations of autumn powder that illuminated ski trails among the gray aspens.

It wasn't just the scenery. I expected the people to be territorial snots, but they weren't. They were open and full of fun. I took a room at a hotel with the difficult name of Gasthof Gramshammer (after a couple of Coors, it comes out as Gashouse Grandslammer) and then walked along fast-flowing Gore Creek to Glenn Lokay's tackle shop. It was the day before the Ironman, and Lokay, with his Yosemite Sam mustache and malamute eyes, was holding a meeting for contestants. I'd assumed the place would be jammed with *A River Runs Through It* types. Instead, only about a dozen men and women, mostly Colorado guides, milled through the shop, passing a pint of whiskey around and occasionally spitting Copenhagen loogies out the door.

Typical, I thought. Even so, I had to give the local guides credit. There was not a swollen ego among them. Since the actual fishing would be my weakest event, I was touched when several of them went way out of their way to help me choose a fly and leader for the one-fly fish-off. I also had to give Lokay credit. Despite the short notice, he'd wangled some big-ticket prizes—gorgeous Sage fly rods and a superb Abel reel among them. By the end of the meeting I felt penitent for my sweeping judgments of these amiable people. Maybe I was befuddled by the Jim Beam, maybe it was the damn snuff they fed me, but I began to wonder if it wasn't I who was the territorial snot.

The next day, though, the morning of the Ironman, I felt better— steely and full of competitive fire. More like my old self. After all, I hadn't come to this mountain paradise to have fun. It was Lokay who reminded me of the date: Friday the thirteenth. "Good luck," he said, smiling. "You're going to need it."

Over the years Vail has hosted a garden variety of national and international competitions, not to mention Gerald Ford and

Princess Di, but never had the village accommodated an event so outlandish as the Ironman Fly-fishing Championship of the World. That's what I was thinking as I stood in my underwear on the ninth fairway of the Vail Country Club, alternately ducking golf balls and cursing the bastards who whacked them at us.

"Ignore those linksters," Lokay instructed us. "I knew they'd behave like this. Like they *own* the place."

The sky was a bright, glacial blue. There were eleven of us carrying fly rods, ten men and one woman making practice casts, warming up for the first two events: distance casting and golf. I wore a partisan banner in the form of red Florida State Seminole boxer shorts over an old green wrestling singlet. Several of the other contestants wore long johns, a prissy concession to the October chill, I believed, and a symptom of weak character.

I was feeling confident. One reason was that I *knew* I was going to win the distance casting. I knew it not because I was the best caster there—frankly, I wasn't—but because a friend of mine, Professor Bruce Richards of Scientific Anglers, had sent me by FedEx a high-tech fly line that I had consistently thrown 130 feet the afternoon before. (I'd mention the type of line, but some of you are unethical enough to use it against me next year.)

Another reason I felt confident was that I had persuaded a buddy of mine, Bobby Cox, to sign up for the competition. A former member of the NHL's Chicago Blackhawks, Cox's journeyman career carried him to every third-rate hockey rink from Stockholm to Kiev, where he slashed capitalist and Commie defensemen with equal impunity and earned a dark reputation and a darker nickname: Side Show Bob. Were the world orderly and rational, scientists would have darted Cox like a bear and kept him under observation for years before releasing him back into the wild. But the world is neither, and Cox, now in his midforties, has parlayed his contacts and his gift for languages into international holdings and a reputation as a financial wizard.

Cox knew nothing about fly fishing, but he was going to be my key to winning the river run. As we stood on the ninth fairway, I told him, "I'll win the distance casting, I should place in the golf and the accuracy. The costume competition is anybody's guess. Say, how do I look?"

"Idiotic. Like a KGB agent who robbed a circus."

"Perfect. Then I've got a chance—as long as you play blocker for me during the river run. No one gets past you, understand? No one. Except for me, of course."

Cox wobbled the fly rod he was holding. "How the hell am I supposed to hurt anybody with this? It's not even sharp. You told me fly fishing was fun."

"Hockey has given you a wonderfully quirky approach to life, Side Show," I said. "But your secret is safe with me. Just get the job done."

Trouble was, I didn't get the job done. Not in the distance casting, anyway. I placed a miserable fifth, casting only ninety-some feet. But there was a legitimate reason for my sad performance. Some doofus was standing on my line when I made my cast: me, the doofus.

I placed third in the costume contest, however, and then rallied for the golf competition, which took place on a hundred-yard par five with a nasty dogleg right. I managed to bogey the hole, as did Mike "Poodle Head" Moser and Mike Paderewski. These two Gore Creek guides would prove to be my strongest competition, although I kicked their respective butts during the eighty-yard, closest-to-the-pin shoot-out to win the golf event.

It was at about that point in the competition that Vail guide Jimmy Garrett began to ply the leaders with strong drink. For that reason the next few events are a blur, although I remember I was accused of cheating during the blindfolded knot tying and, as expected, I didn't do too well in the actual one-fly fish-off, catching only two tiny rainbows.

I also recall that as we moved from event to event, we began to acquire a crowd of onlookers and then media coverage, which in Lokay's mind boded well for next year's Ironman. This I was glad to see. Lokay had been dispirited by my morning successes. "The Ironman will be compromised if a chum-slinger like you places higher than ninth," he had told me, but the media attention seemed to buoy his mood. "Even your freakish luck can't dent this thing's momentum," he now chided me.

What I remember best, though, is the river run, officially known as the Boxer Speed Spawn. The standings had Poodle Head Moser in first place and me close on his heels in second. If I could manage a win in the river run, and if Poodle Head did poorly, I would be Ironman Fly-fishing Champion of the World. The course was intimidating: up the Eagle River to a sand spit, then across through a chest-deep swale, and then back, all in near-freezing water.

As we lined the bank, awaiting the start, I nudged Cox, winked at him, and said, "Pretend we're on the blue line and you've got to stop every Russian in the world from beating you to the goal."

A strange and terrible light came into the man's eyes. "Russians?" he whispered. "You . . . *you* look like a Russian." Which is when the gun sounded and Side Show Bobby Cox paused only long enough to yank my underwear to my ankles before he splashed off to victory in a rage of elbows and head butts, beating every man and woman there, most of whom were half his age.

Later, he came to his senses while I was inspecting my second-place prize, the Able reel. Cox apologized and then he said, "You're right, fly fishing is fun."

PARADISE FOULED

On my return to what was once the best place in the world, I was reminded of an elemental dilemma that attends anyone who seeks out remote, unspoiled places and then writes about them for profit—a carrion feeder's ethic that has motivated me and others to foul our own nests more than once. It might have been Western Australia, or it might have been Borneo, or it might have been a variety of other small, private places, but it happened to be Costa Rica, where the reminder first came in the form of a noxious little shyster who wore the blue uniform of that tiny country's transit police.

His name was Barrantes. He wore mirrored sunglasses. His swagger insinuated a yearning for the firearm he was not allowed to carry. He moved slowly, very, very slowly. His authority mandated that my time was his time; it was his small power to wield.

He approached my rental car, slapping a little citation booklet against his hand. He gave me a look—contempt, perhaps?—before informing me in Spanish that his radar gun had clocked my speed at eighty kilometers per hour in a sixty-kph zone.

His mood didn't improve when I told him my Spanish wasn't very good.

"Eighty kilometers an hour!" he said. "You don't understand *that*?"

Well, yeah, I did. But why was this twerp hollering at me? Maybe it was true that I had been doing the equivalent of forty-eight miles per hour in a thirty-six-mph zone, but it was also true that I had been driving on a busy three-lane highway and was being passed by other cars when I topped the ridge and saw Barrantes standing on the curb, aiming his radar gun. Yet mine was the only car he had flagged.

"You want trouble? You have big trouble!" The guy was leaning into the car window, lecturing me in English. "You pay fine now. Pay now or I arrest you maybe!"

Gad! Was I in Costa Rica or back in Cuba? Or maybe Mexico, where a *federale* shakedown is budgeted into every trip? When one travels a lot, the mind sometimes blurs. I took a look around: tropical mountains hazed with blue, coffee bushes hedge-neat on hillsides, houses roofed with red tile. Nope, this was definitely Costa Rica.

"You don't pay, we go back to San José!" Infuriated by my silence, Barrantes was now leveraging me with threats. I shook my head. Nope, I wasn't going to hand over American dollars. I'd take the ticket and pay later.

Barrantes slapped his hand with the citation booklet a final time. "You big trouble!" Then he sauntered back to his vehicle, letting me know through body language that he would keep me waiting as long as he could.

With me in the car was my fifteen-year-old son, Lee. I turned and asked, "What'd I do to make him so mad?"

"It's because we're in a rental car," said Lee. "Don't you remember what Bayardo told us? They like to stop rental cars." The voice of calm and reason from a calmer, more reasonable person, and he was right.

Bayardo had warned me—Bayardo Orochena, a Nicaraguan national who was manager of San José's Hotel Balmoral. Bayardo was an old buddy of mine and had watched my infant sons grow to childhood during our annual visits to Costa Rica. I had written about the astonishing flora and fauna of this West Virginia–size country and the friendliness of its people, had marveled in print at a place where one could watch howler monkeys on the Pacific Coast in the morning and quetzals in the cloud forest at noon and still arrive in the Caribbean lowlands in time to see a three-toed sloth or an American crocodile. As I and many other writers and photographers discovered early on, the natural wealth of Costa Rica was an indulgence that could be had for the price of sharing it.

"Why's he taking so long?" Lee was getting restless. It had been more than seven years since we had been to Costa Rica, and it was our plan to revisit our favorite place, the place where our family had spent so much time. Sitting in the sweltering heat and the wind wake of passing cars wasn't supposed to be part of the plan.

I could see Barrantes in the rearview mirror, loitering with another officer, the partially finished ticket clasped in his hand. Years earlier I had written, "Put these kindly Costa Ricans behind the wheel of a car and they become aggressive, wild, filled with a crazy faith in life after death."

It was true. Costa Rica had once been a world leader in traffic fatalities. Because road carnage and the publicity it generated was bad for tourism, the Policia de Transito had been created to snuff out the problem. Soon I would learn that the PDT's greed and corruption are symptomatic of other problems that have gradually moved in to fill the void.

To Lee, I said, "He thinks that if he waits here long enough, I'll pay him. He wants a bribe."

"The guy's a jerk."

"Yeah."

"Did you ever have to do that before?"

I answered, "Pay bribes? In other places. Not here. Never here."

The best place in the world was where Bern, the cook, died unexpectedly in the night. By the time the Cessna landed to mule him out, he was so stiff that we had to lever his body into the front seat and leave the door slightly ajar for an arm that refused to bend. As the airplane taxied away, it appeared that Bern was waving farewell to us, a cavalier gesture that was very much in character.

The best place in the world was where Jesus, with his crippled hand, led my toddler sons through a tunnel of pandanus palms and mangoes in search of iguanas. It was where pretty Marielena, in her flowered skirt, oiled the black wood of the ranch house porch every morning and brought me avocado sandwiches or bottles of cold Tropical beer anytime I wanted.

It was where we had to saddle roping ponies and ride two miles of deserted beach to buy lobster in the village of Tambor or to hang out at Momo's Bar in Pochote. It was where I could sit quietly and read while my auburn-haired wife slept in a wide hammock, a blond son and a redheaded son curled beneath each arm. It was where the jungle met the sea, a place where, summer after summer, I could be alone with my loves and watch them change against the backdrop of rain-tree green and Pacific gray that were the colors of an unchanging Costa Rica.

The best place in the world had a name. It was La Hacienda, a cattle ranch on the Peninsula of Nicoya, fronting Bahía Ballena, the Bay of Whales.

Most of my lucky travel discoveries have resulted from misadventure, a poor sense of geography, and blind good fortune. La Hacienda was no different. I was staying in San José with my wife, Debra, and Lee, who was then two, and we decided to roam. We took a bus to the dirty port town of Puntarenas, where we saw an ad for a boat tour. We got on the boat. It was a blustery day, and a guy on board was smoking a cigar. My pregnant wife got sick. Lee got queasy. I had the skipper drop us off at the closest landfall— the village of Paquera. I believed that we could find a bus to take us back to San José. The villagers chuckled at me as I made inquiries. Had I not looked at a map?

What I found was a man who introduced himself as Bayardo Orochena. Bayardo had come with a stake-bed truck to carry supplies from the ferry. He told me that he was managing a cattle ranch that sometimes doubled as an inn and that he would gladly take us there—if we didn't mind riding in the back of his truck.

We rode for nearly an hour over mud trails, crabbing our way up and down hills, past little villages where bird-of-paradise plants and parrots grew wild. Finally we mounted a ridge. Below were coconut palms growing on a strand of black beach that abutted pasturelands on the Pacific. We turned toward the sea, and I got my first look at La Hacienda.

Years ago, I wrote about it: "The main house is constructed of heavy wood and red tile, with broad porches and hammocks on grounds so perfectly kept that it is as if someone has transported a botanical garden to the seventh fairway of Augusta Country Club. There are hedges of hibiscus in big red bloom where hummingbirds compete with bees. Everywhere else you look there is nothing but water and jungle and beach. It is a cattle ranch with ocean at its front and mountains at its back."

My family and I planned to stay a night. We stayed a week. It was embarrassingly inexpensive. We went back every summer after that. Rarely were there any other guests. In the mornings my wife, a gifted runner, would vanish down the beach. I would head the opposite way on horseback, my fly rod braced against my thigh like a Winchester.

There was no television, so the evenings required conversation. Bayardo was a brilliant conversationalist. He could talk about politics or business or romance with equal expertise. Because the ranch had no electricity, we would sit on the porch long after the generator had been switched off, listening to frogs and ducking bats drawn to the oil lamps.

I got to know Bern, the German cook, who beat me regularly at chess right up until the day the Cessna came to fetch him. Jesus became a favorite of my sons, Marielena became a favorite of us all, and I became buddies with Momo, owner of Momo's Bar, and spent more than one afternoon trying to teach him how to juggle.

What I remember best is how Marielena and the other women would all sob when we left La Hacienda, reaching to stroke the soft hair of our sons.

While others wrote about the cloud forests of Monte Verde or the turtles of Tortuguero or the volcanoes of northern Costa Rica, I wrote about the Peninsula of Nicoya. My rationalization was also a truth: I was sharing. That is the small conceit and larger dishonesty embraced by people who do what I do.

So it had been seven years. Because of busy schedules, we missed a summer at La Hacienda, and another summer. Then, when I called, I was told that the ranch was no longer open to paying guests. It was a surprising thing to hear.

Finally, I tracked down Bayardo. His intellect and his gift for business had catapulted him from ranch manager to manager of the comfortable Hotel Balmoral in downtown San José. He told me that La Hacienda had been sold to a Spanish conglomerate that planned to build a new resort on the Bay of Whales.

"Maybe it will happen, maybe it won't," he said. "Even if it does, I have other places for us to go. Places just as pretty. Costa Rica is still one of the most beautiful countries in the world."

That much was true, even seven years later. The only thing different that I noticed as Lee and I drove from San José through mountains and green valleys was the marked increase in traffic. In recent years, Costa Rica has become a hot ticket for travelers from the United States and Europe. Ecotourism has joined coffee as the country's primary cash cow. We heard a lot more English spoken—and German, too. We saw a lot more signs hawking rafting trips and fishing excursions and birding tours. The pace of the place had quickened, become more competitive, and some of the locals we met and re-met had been changed by it.

The shyster transit cop was an extreme example, but avarice is tourism's ugly stepchild. (When I paid the ticket back in San José, the rental car company charged me an attorney fee—their own little chunk of the extortion business.)

Puntarenas was still cheerful and dirty. We drove onto the ferry and, an hour later, exited onto the Peninsula of Nicoya and the village of Paquera. Much of the road to Tambor had been paved. It was a much quicker trip, though it seemed longer because I was confused by all the changes. There were houses now—not many, but a few—big houses on hillsides that had the flavor of overseas money.

We topped a ridge, and suddenly I could see the Bay of Whales: jungled bluffs rising out of a gray sea.

"That's what I remember," Lee said. "How pretty it is."

That's what I remembered, too. Even so, we were nearly to Tambor before I realized that I had completely missed the entrance to La Hacienda. We backtracked. I still couldn't find it. Off to the right was a wide cement driveway and a little guardhouse. A sign read BARCELO PLAYA TAMBOR BEACH RESORT.

I pulled in, and the guard told me what I already suspected: this was the entrance. Could we drive in and look around? No, but if we were interested in staying at the resort, he could radio the main office and ask permission for us to go in and speak with a clerk.

Playa Tambor Beach Resort was a stationary cruise ship spread out over what was once pasture and empty beach. There were nearly twenty big, modern, Caribbean-style buildings, which included 402 twin-bed rooms and all the maintenance and support infrastructure such a sprawling complex requires. There were three restaurants, three bars, a disco, a casino, and a small shopping mall. The resort offered classes in tennis, aerobics, scuba, sailing, windsurfing, whitewater rafting, and riding. At the center, fronting the beach, was a three-tiered chickee hut the size of a football field. Beside it was the "largest swimming pool in Central America," a series of lagoons, waterfalls, and cement lakes a shade of lucent jade that was penetrating if one looked from the sea to the pool too quickly.

Lee liked the pool. I could tell.

"You want to stay?"

"It's pretty nice."

"I'll go register. After that, anything you want to eat, anything you want to use, just ask for it. The price includes it all."

That afternoon, in a misting drizzle, I walked the beach and found La Hacienda. The windows had been boarded and plugged with air-conditioning units. The hammocks were gone; the black wood of the porch was scuffed raw. It was now housing for resort employees.

I stood there staring, feeling the rain, feeling proportionately reduced by the perception that it seemed smaller. It was naive to believe that my stories had caused the destruction of this remote place. Mine was but one small voice in a larger chorus, yet I had participated in the process, and it was not a pleasant thing to concede.

There is an issue that we who do what we do prefer to disregard: too often we diminish the places we most love. We can brandish rationalizations, we can even cling to the truth that sometimes we also contribute in certain ways to the protection and economic well-being of fragile regions. Even so, the dilemma remains. This might have been Western Australia, or it might have been Borneo, or it might have been any of the dozens of far-flung places that I've enjoyed privately and helped make public, but it wasn't.

This was my place, La Hacienda.

As I walked toward the house, iguanas rattled beneath pandanus palms and mango trees. I stopped at the steps as a door to one of the rooms peeked open. Someone spoke, a woman's voice: did I require assistance? Did I realize that I was in a place not available to guests? The door opened wider.

It was Marielena, though it was a long moment before I realized it. She wore the white uniform of kitchen help and a net over her hair. She had gained twenty-some pounds. Like me, she had aged.

First, we shook hands; then we hugged, but briefly, very briefly. Hers was the nervous reserve of someone not permitted to fraternize with customers. She kept glancing over her shoulder as if someone might see us. It was not easy to get her to talk, but I wanted to know what had happened, who was where.

Familiar names were spoken in a rush: Jesus, she said, was now a gardener for a rich man on the mainland. His brother, Fidel, was a waiter at Playa Tambor—perhaps he would wait on me tonight! Beautiful Daisy, the teenager who wore the hibiscus in her hair and helped with the floors, was gone; she didn't know where. But Momo still owned his bar, although he quit drinking several years ago.

"He now drives a beautiful gold car," Marielena told me, wondering if she should be impressed.

It was a Range Rover. I would see it the next night when I drove to Pochote. Momo would take one look at me and begin to juggle invisible balls in the air.

"And what about your wife and your two sons?" Marielena's question was sincere, but she was also anxious for me to be gone, eager for the distance that her position now required.

I thought of Lee and told her that I had a surprise for her—but tomorrow, at the resort. Such reintroductions were risky, here at the best place in the world. Marielena would only have cried.

THE INVISIBLE ORANGUTANS OF BORNEO

Trained scientist that he is, a physician buddy of mine, while standing in the gloom of an Indonesian rain forest, recently touched upon a key irony of middle age when he paused to reflect: "You know, Rando, every problem I've ever had in my life has started with this little son of a bitch."

I was immediately interested. "Which son of a bitch?" I asked him. "Where? Let me see."

I'd been searching the high tree canopy, hoping to spot an orangutan or maybe a macaque, but instantly turned eyes toward my friend. Maybe he was referring to a tick or some kind of rare toad. But no . . . the man was urinating against the planked base of a gigantic tree, culprit in hand—bilging ship as those of us who are ticketed boat captains refer to it. "Gad!" I told him, moving away. "Don't ever trick me like that again!"

But he wasn't done. "It's no joke," he said. "If it wasn't for this bastard, I'd be a wealthy man. The thing's cost me about a hundred thousand dollars an inch—the only time in my life I've been eager to underestimate. Plus a beautiful house. He's caused me months of sleepless nights. It's ruined two marriages, alienated me from my only child, wasted more of my professional time than I want to believe, and consumed more creative energy than I care to admit."

He added, "I find that old cliché 'A stiff prick has no conscience' offensive and demeaning. Worse, it's inaccurate. I'm a thoughtful human being. I care about women as people. I recognize the importance of moral standards. I've had many, many invitations to be unfaithful from every kind of woman—many of them supposedly 'happily' married. Yet I've acted on fewer than one, maybe two percent of those opportunities. Women say we're hounds? They're just as promiscuous but more purposeful. We screw like scavengers. They screw like snipers. All that said, the little son of a bitch has come *this* close to destroying my life more than once."

After another thoughtful pause, the doctor said, "I think nature gave the bugger a plumbing fuction to create the illusion of control. Seriously, every penis should be stamped with a warning like a cigarette package or something. CAUTION: JUST BECAUSE YOU CAN AIM IT DOESN'T MEAN YOU'RE IN COMMAND."

No argument there.

It was a valid point and appropriate not only to our respective lives but also to our current location. We were hiking the outskirt trails of Sepilok Orangutan Rehabilitation Center near the port city of Sandakan, northern Borneo. Borneo is the third-largest island in the world and among my favorite places. For reasons that are as complicated as they are interesting (border wars, Commie rabble, and white rajas all played roles), Borneo has been carved into three politically separate entities. Indonesia controls the central and southern portion while Malaysia controls all of the north, with the exception of Brunei, a tiny, oil-rich sultanate that has few roads but bunches of Rolls-Royces. In Borneo, the food is exotic, the markets are fascinating, and the wildlife is varied.

I was there on a quest of sorts, determined to come to terms with this hellbroth known as middle age. After a couple of contemplative weeks in Australia, I'd rendezvoused with my doctor buddy in Kota Kinabalu—my second visit to Borneo in the last few years. (On an earlier trip, I'd traveled with a thoracic surgeon. A rule of thumb in choosing traveling companions: for Third World countries, recruit physicians; for the United States and Canada, invite lawyers. Pharmaceuticals and writs can be invaluable in an emergency situation.) This friend was a noted orthopedist from a northern state with lots of vowels. He, too, was attempting to make peace with recent changes in his life. Clearly, infidelity had played a damaging role.

"Let me give you an example of how sex dominates lives—" he said.

I interrupted him. "I'm not going to listen to a word until you've finished what you're doing."

I meant it. I can't explain why, but obvious vulnerability undermines credibility. There were distracting canine implications, plus it's impossible to take a man seriously while he's pissing on a tree. After a few more seconds, when he'd zipped, he said, "Let's use Washington as a case in point."

"Sure," I replied. "D.C." I was searching the high canopy again. To see or hear great apes in the wild is one of the most powerful things I've ever experienced, and I was eager to make contact.

"Washington has a superb zoo," the doctor said. "In that zoo are a number of gorillas. The most powerful male gorilla is rewarded with the sexual devotion of every female around. A male gorilla's strength is defined by the number of females he copulates with. Same is true with all primates, from orangutans on down. You following me so far?"

"Perfectly," I replied. My mind was unusually clear, perhaps because beer is outrageously expensive in Borneo—as much as $6 U.S. per bottle. It was fiscally imprudent to overserve oneself. On the other hand, maybe the many beery nights I'd spent in

Australia had weeded out some of my weak brain cells. The feeble die first—it's a primary law of natural selection. While in Oz, I'd done some serious cell culling.

The doctor pressed on: "Not far from the D.C. Zoo is the White House. The man who lives there is the most powerful man in the world. Like most of us, it's taken him years to rise to the peak of his powers, yet his *weakness* is defined by the number of females he has copulated with. You see the irony of that? We are the only primate on earth obligated to live contrary to our own genetic coding. Do you understand my point?"

It was now safe to confront the man eye to eye, so I did. "Look," I told him, "I'm no fan of Bill's. If we were invited on the same canoe trip, I'd take the bus and only leave to eat. But if you think I'm going to stand here and listen to you accuse the president of the United States of screwing gorillas, you're barking up the wrong tree, mister. Even I refuse to believe that one."

Yes, I'd deflected his sincerity with a joke. It's what we do when confronted with an uncomfortable truth, and my friend was confronting an uncomfortable truth, indeed: the more successful we are by the time we reach middle age, the more likely we are to foul up our lives with sex.

My doctor buddy had seldom conceded to the drive yet had lost much. My own life was not without complexities. We were both laughing, but it was wistful laughter, the kind that squeezes the heart. In light of our circumstances, in view of the pain the drive had caused ourselves and so many others, there was only one other reasonable reaction. But what would either of us gain from crying?

The subject came to dominate our Borneo trip. We discussed it while we roamed the Central Market on Tun Fuad Street, marveling at tubs of water buffalo tongue, live fruit bats with six-foot wingspans (they were sold as aphrodisiacs), wild honey, turtle eggs, dog haunches, and other strange wares for sale. We debated it while my friend Hial Esten and his little homemade boat sped us up the Kinabatangan River, a conduit of yellow water that augered its way into the jungle abyss.

We were still looking for a glimpse of wild orangutans. There was a reason: once, camped on the Alas River in the mountains of Sumatra, I'd listened to two tribes of black gibbons—small gorillas—taunt each other from the safety of opposite banks of the river. That sound, that haunting sound, vibrated in my abdomen. It had an electrical resonance. Unlike any sound I'd ever heard before or since, it was translated first by the fight-or-flight instinct and, only then, was entrusted to the intellect. I'd felt a similar charge when the thoracic surgeon and I, in Borneo, had stumbled upon a female orangutan and her two young in the rain forest. I was determined to make that connection again, but orangutans are among the shyest of the great apes.

We were always on the search.

Question: what do Bob Packwood, Gary Hart, Congressman Phillip Crane, Henry Cisneros, Barney Frank, Marv Albert, Frank Gifford, Wade Boggs, and Big Jefe (Big Chief) Bill Clinton have in common? We asked ourselves that.

And we answered: they are all intelligent, successful men who, upon occasion, have provided much-needed leadership and comfort to the rest of us by proving that we are not the only middle-aged dumb asses who occasionally behave like lobotomy survivors.

Question: why do successful men, no matter what age, attract women, lots of women?

And we answered: because Henry Kissinger was right—power is the greatest aphrodisiac.

I had another question for my well-read doctor buddy: "What do psychiatrists, behaviorial experts—those kinds of people— have to say on the subject?"

His answer was surprising but from the heart. "They know just about as much as you know about brain surgery. Hell, less, because they attempt to linearize what is nonlinear. They hide behind these idiotic labels: 'sexual addiction,' 'extreme narcissism,' 'self-validation.' What baloney. It's all designed to defuse responsibility. Rational people accept what is rational: we're all accountable for our own behavior. Our lives our simpler and healthier if we are faithful to one person, but we screw around anyway. Most of us fight the instinct, most of us fail. Excuses are a device. If you want the truth about why we behave the way we do, you're more likely to find it in the locker room. Or the dugout."

Coincidentally, I had recently played in a men's senior baseball world series and had assembled stories of sexual infidelity—from amateurs and former pros alike—with the expectations of using the tales in this column. But good sense got the best of me and I abandoned the idea: any lowlife who would betray a locker room confidence under the guise of journalism is an asshole and should receive the whipping he richly deserves. Men's lives and careers are not to be toyed with. But one afternoon, lounging around the pool of Sandakan's five-star Renaissance Hotel, my doctor buddy and I compared notes and compiled not only what we felt were the most tragic tales of infidelity, but also some rules of conduct for anyone dumb enough to fall prey to the behavior.

Tragic tales: the orthopedic surgeon who, the morning after breaking up with his mistress, was deep into a patient's hip, installing a steel pin, when nurses arrived consecutively with unhappy news: (1) the mistress was in the emergency room having unsuccessfully attempted suicide; (2) the wife, after being contacted by the distraught mistress, was in the emergency room having unsuccessfully tried suicide. During the hellish updates that followed, the distraught surgeon lost control of the steel pin and the pin ended up in the patient's stomach. The surgeon had to wait while an internist was called in and operated—succesfully.

"If the poor bastard had had two mistresses instead of one," my doctor buddy told me, "the frigging pin would have ended up in the patient's throat. Thank God urology wasn't involved."

Fifteen or sixteen other tragic tales: men who lured or who were lured into bed by the decent, faithful "never promiscuous" friends of friends or the wives of friends and who ended up giving their own wives a venereal disease.

"There are far more immaculate infections than there are immaculate conceptions," my doctor buddy told me. "Of course women, like men, never lie to bedmates, particularly married women. So there's no explanation for the way these viruses are spread."

Was he being facetious?

"Uh-h-h-h, yes," he said. "I'm being facetious."

Which is why we compiled a short code of behavior for men at risk:

1. Choose one good woman and be faithful.
2. If you stumble and are unfaithful, forgive yourself. It's the guilt that kills us, and feeling guilty for acting upon a genetic drive is akin to feeling guilty for being stocky.
3. If the woman you are with does not accept that fact, admit nothing. Use BJ Bill's outrageous lie: like hidden data about UFOs, it's all a conspiracy.
4. Better yet, have her visit the D.C. Zoo.
5. If you have committed yourself to a good woman, do not, under any circumstances, allow yourself to fall in love with another woman.
6. If you fall in love, remember this inviolate truth: one way or another, it will not end happily.

7. The terms *soul mate* and *spiritual partner* are effective in infomercials thumping psychic hot lines, but they are an illusion in all other respects. Remind yourself: your "soul mate" found guys to sleep with before she met you; she'll find guys to sleep with after you're gone.

8. Your children are your only true soul mates.

9. If you want to leave the woman you're with, but don't have the courage to do it cleanly, be man enough not to subject her to the systematic destructive cycle that is designed to make your unhappiness appear as "her fault." It's not her fault, it's not your fault. It's the way you feel, and you have nothing to be ashamed of.

10. We have a right to be happy.

Happy, yes . . . like the orangutans we were seeking.

"At a certain stage in their lives," my doctor buddy told me, "the mature males go off by themselves and live alone. They are among the shyest, most reclusive primates on earth. But you never know—we might see one."

We never did.

'COON HUNT

On a night in which much interaction with dogs and raccoons was anticipated, Shane Groves and his buddy Vandardis Black took the time to counsel me as to why it was necessary that other creatures be involved, namely two animals that were referred to as "mules" but, in fact, resembled mutant peccaries.

"There they are," Shane said, pointing. "You ever ridden anything like them before?"

Nope. I'd never ridden anything like them before. It was possible that I'd never even seen anything like them before—hard to tell because visibility wasn't good. It was the darkest sort of night: October in the northwest corner of Ohio where autumn starlight rattles through the wind as it is absorbed by corn stubble.

"You won't regret it," Shane told me. He meant having a mule to ride. "Out there in the woods, chasing those dogs through the briers and the trees, you'll be real happy about having a mule."

I was unconvinced. Chasing dogs through briers and trees seemed diversion enough.

We were at the T. L. Brown farm on County Road O, just southeast of the village of Pioneer and not too far from Kunkle, which is west of Aldvorton but well north of Cooney and

Hicksville—grange towns you won't find in most atlases, but might on a really good road map. From the aspect of an air corridor thirty thousand feet above, this region would appear to jet travelers as an expanding darkness interspersed by frail colonies of light; lights that mark the night strongholds of human existence in all rural places. It is what certain hot-shot types in New York and L.A. refer to as "fly-over" country—a term that trivializes the Midwest while insinuating a social superiority that no outsider who has ever been to New York or L.A. takes seriously. That term, and all that it implies, was one of the reasons that I was now standing at the corral gate of the T. L. Brown farm, peering through the gloom at what appeared to be several elephant-size horses, among which stood the two mutant peccaries.

"Are those Clydesdales?" I asked.

Shane, sixteen and a junior at North Central High in Pioneer, was busy gathering ropes and harnesses. "Nope, I already told you. They're mules." Clearly, the kid was focused on his quarry and assumed that I was too.

"Not the little ones," I said. "The really big ones."

"Huh? Nope, those aren't Clydesdales, those are Belgians. They're draft *horses*. We take them around to fairs and enter them in pulling contests. Ohio, Michigan, Illinois. Everywhere. We got one can pull a forty-five-hundred-pound sled. It's what we do when we're not busy 'coon hunting. Or running our snowmobiles. Or fishing. But those Belgians, they wouldn't be any good at all at chasing dogs. Dog makes one wrong step . . . squish. Heck, if *we* made a wrong step—squish!"

I found his reply heartening. For one thing, I didn't want to be squished. For another, it meant I wouldn't have to try to climb aboard one of those monster animals. Finally, it doubly validated my pet theory—the theory that had brought me to Pioneer, Ohio. It was my belief that no matter where a visitor happened to land in fly-over country, the visitor would discover that interesting, high-energy people were busy doing interesting things in outdoor places that might not be as photogenic as Aspen or as exotic as Maui, but were just as valuable in terms of interacting with nature not to mention kick-butt fun.

"Hold the gate while we catch Sass and Tom."

The mules had names. Sean and Vandardis tethered them and led them out. When distanced from the draft horses, the animals seemed to grow in stature until they, for once, assumed the appearance of things found on a farm rather than in the Amazon basin. Not that they were classic representatives of the breed. Sass looked as if the DNA helix of more than one foul-tempered pony was clogging its gene pool. Tom, who was much bigger, had glazed, surly eyes, as if its forebears might have run amok of the Belgians and the resultant grudge now transcended generations.

"You want to help load these mules?" Vandardis was speaking to me.

No, I didn't want to help load these mules. Their demeanor didn't invite familiarity. More to the point, it was my guess that both animals bit like dogs. But I helped anyway, pushing, pulling, and leveraging Tom and Sass into the horse trailer while Shane reviewed our plans for the evening. After we loaded the mules and the dogs, he said, we'd drive back into Pioneer to pick up lights and gear, then we'd truck and trailer the animals across into Michigan, where he and Vandardis knew of a woods loaded with raccoons.

"The kind of place that 'coon hunting's all about," Shane said.

That's why I was with Shane and Vandardis—we were going 'coon hunting. According to Shane, we would loose the dogs in a likely spot, then stand around beneath the stars and listen to the dogs bark. From the inflection of their yapping, Shane and Vandardis would know when the dogs were on trail, when the dogs were closing in on a 'coon, and when the dogs had a 'coon treed. That's when we would leap upon the mules and ride pell-mell through the briers and the trees.

"Then you shoot the raccoon?" I asked Shane.

He seemed mildly surprised by the question, but the kid was a diplomat. "Well . . . we could shoot them; yeah, I suppose we could. But we won't, because that would make just one less 'coon for the next time we go out, right? No, the reason we're doing what we're doing is to work the dogs; train them how to track 'coons. The dogs love it, the mules don't seem to mind, and I'm beginning to think the 'coons get a kick out of it too. Don't they, Vandardis?"

Vandardis Black was nodding. "The way they look down when the dogs have them treed, it's like, 'Hey—we'll get even. Leave your trash out and you'll be sorry.' Or—'We know where your sweet corn lives.'"

"It's like that," Shane said. "Understand?"

I was beginning to.

Shane added, "See, we enter the dogs in 'coon dog trials. Take them all over the place—Ohio, Michigan, Illinois. You name it. When we're not pulling the Belgians at fairs. Or running our snowmobiles. Like I told you. Or fishing. Believe me, you're about to have the wildest time in your life. Running dogs through the woods at night on mule-back is pretty much a guaranteed good time."

I was beginning to understand that, too.

Truth is, I'd been having a very good time ever since I and my rental car left the dinge of Detroit International Airport and escaped south into fly-over country. The village of Pioneer, just two miles beyond the Michigan border and only 15 miles from the Indiana line, seemed an ideal destination. I liked the implications of its name, *Pioneer*—indigenous and European peoples who settled what is now the Midwest had defined the word. Also, because Pioneer was wedged between the borders of two other fly-over states, it had a geographical resonance that suggested wider representation: it might be any small town between Nebraska and Pennsylvania. If Pioneer's thousand-plus residents were out there having fun, hip-deep in nature and God knows what else, then there was no reason for the Midwest to warrant indifference, let alone play ugly stepchild to every recreational glamour attraction from sea to shining sea. I was in an investigatory frame of mind. Adventure is my business, and I was on a mission.

I crossed the Ohio line on State Route 15, and Pioneer emerged from a gray horizon: winterized houses, water tower elevated above an island of trees, sidewalks, mossy brick buildings by a solitary traffic light at the village center. To my right was Hometown Hardware, to my left was Sooz's Restaurant, which was just across from the one-room library. I spoke with the librarian. "People in this county love to read, but there're lots of other things to do," she promised. I tracked down Pioneer's mayor, Alan Fiser, who also runs the local bank. "This is a solid, progressive little town," he told me. "You won't find a better place to raise children. Everything we do revolves around our kids. Our high school has a great choir, good cultural events, and excellent teachers. If you want to find active people, stop at the high school."

I found the school—North Central High—set among elms and October maples on Baubice Street. The mayor was mayor for a reason. He knew his town. In a school of eight hundred students, kindergarten through twelfth, nearly every teacher I met had his or her own enthusiastic outdoor agenda—and the kids were usually included. Did I want to do a cross-country run? What about mountain biking? The county had no mountains, but there were plenty of tractor trails to ride. Or I could drive to Lake La Su An, a state park, and fly fish. Or there were some bird-watchers around, although spring was a better time, but autumn was ideal for astronomy because of the clear skies and almost no light pollution.

But it was school librarian Sherry Shipley, a take-charge woman, who ultimately captured me—there is no other way to describe it—and helped fix my itinerary. Shipley is one of those people whose biorhythms are synched to a faster, brighter current. She sweeps bystanders along by force of enthusiasm, and those who tarry are grabbed by the arm and yanked. Shipley grabbed my arm and yanked more than once. What I *might* do, Shipley told me, was take English teacher Maxine Pulver's suggestion and go 'coon hunting with some of the students. And since the students hunted raccoons at night, what I *could* do is spend the day on a canoe exploratory with Shipley's husband, Tom.

"With all the creeks and rivers in this county," she told me, "a lot of people are saying we need a canoe trail. Maybe you guys can find a good section to get it started."

We guys had our orders. I met Tom the next afternoon and followed his gray pickup truck to a place on the St. Joseph River where we hid his canoe, then dropped his truck a mile or two away. I guessed we could paddle the distance in forty or fifty minutes. It took us three hours.

The St. Joseph is a narrow farm river, not unlike hundreds of others across the Midwest. Its headwaters are in Michigan, and it flows southwest through Montpelier and Bryan, then on into Indiana, where it joins the St. Mary's and the Maumee Rivers. Not that Tom and I paddled to Indiana—or even to Montpelier. I count myself lucky that we made it to his truck. We put in near a county road bridge and almost immediately had to get out and portage around a barrier of fallen trees. It was the first of many, many portages. We humped the canoe over trees, under trees, and up the steep bank dozens of times. Even so, it was a great paddle. The river was seldom more than thirty feet wide, yet it had cut a deep vein through the earth. There was a subterranean feel to the thing as we followed it along through soft switchbacks, tunneling beneath sycamores and poplars. The current was so sluggish that it was illustrated only by snags, and more than once Tom said, "Here comes another class one rapid."

I liked the fact that the river created the back boundary of farms. On a portage, I could look across plains of soybean or corn stubble and watch people doing chores, futzing with tractors, going about their lives as we moved past silently, anonymously. What I liked best, though, was that the river was a magnet to wildlife. We seldom rounded a bend that we didn't flush wood ducks or quail. Though we saw only one deer, the bank was always a mire of deer tracks, and, high above, Canada geese compassed their way southward, traveling faster than us; faster than I wanted to travel. With a little work, the St. Joe would afford a beautiful canoe trail.

By the time we got to the truck it was already dusk on the river, although the outer world retained an hour of daylight. As we hauled the canoe out, Tom said, "Man, I bet you're pooped. And you still have to go 'coon hunting!"

On the bright side, I'd conserved precious energy by declining invitations to bike the local tractor trails and to run through woods cross-country. Besides, how demanding could 'coon hunting be?

"I'd rather have my son hanging around an oak tree than an oak bar." Shane's father, Mike Groves, told me that while we collected gear from his store, Tri-State Coon Hunters Supply, which is on State Route 15, just south of Pioneer. The store was a marvel of esoteric goods and equipage. There were Nite Stalker lights and Quick Trac ten-channel dog locator systems, stacked bags of Happy Hound dog food, plus a rack of more than 220 outdoor videos, including *Raging Boars, Panfish Power,* and *Corn Crazed*

White Tails. Groves was replying to my observation that not many American fathers would willingly give their sixteen-year-old sons the truck keys along with permission to stay out until 4 A.M. "Shane's a good kid," Mike had said. "He's been hunting the dogs in competitions since he was nine. He's never given me a reason not to trust him."

This was after Shane, Vandardis, and I had loaded the mules, but before we loaded the dogs and drove north into Michigan, where the night seemed to contract, growing darker, and where we stopped, finally, parking in what appeared to be a tractor lane on the east side of a place that Vandardis called the Miller's section. "Lots of 'coons here," Shane said, shutting off the truck. "Let's get the mules unloaded, then we'll cut the dogs loose."

It was no easier to unload the mules than it was to load them. If we pushed, they pulled. When we prodded, they balked. "Darn mules!" Shane yelled at one point. "You don't change your attitudes, I'll leave you back in the barn next time!"

The mules understood, apparently, because neither their attitudes nor their behavior changed.

In contrast, the dogs knew exactly what they were supposed to do, and they did it with a hyperactive enthusiasm. There were two: Toby, a registered redbone, and Suzie, a black-and-tan female. Both hit the ground running, noses to the earth, and disappeared into the woods.

"Now's when the fun starts," Shane said.

"Yeah," said Vandardis. "Listening to the dogs. It's nice."

It was nice, too. The three of us moved away from the truck and sat on the ground. The mules cropped grass nearby. It was a moonless night, no lights anywhere around, and you could peer up through the darkness and see beyond into outer space. While I looked at stars and listened to owls, Shane kept me informed about the dogs. He could tell what was happening by the sound of their voices. "They're just casting now," he said. "Hear them? When they get on a track, they'll let out a locate—the Toby dog will let go with a bawl, then roll it over into a hard chop."

A "bawl" he told me was like a wail; a "chop" was a series of barks.

"Suzie's a good recreational dog," he said, "but it's Toby who will find the line. You wait and see. That Toby dog, he's a registered Night Champion dog. I mean it—through the United Kennel Club. He's a world-class dog worth maybe four thousand dollars, and he always takes the lead. Hear 'im? Hear the bawl? He's on track. They'll have a 'coon treed soon."

The two dogs did have distinctive voices. But I was more interested in the voices of Shane and Vandardis. I listened to them talk about kids at school, and their teachers, then about the coming winter and what the ice fishing would be like. Mostly, though, they spoke of this sport—'coon hunting—and of their favorite woods and of events that made them laugh, and some that didn't, like the night a good three-year-old walker dog, Ringo, came wet out of the swamp, touched an electric fence, and was killed.

"That was a shame," Vandardis said. "That Ringo dog was pretty good, too."

"Yeah, a good dog," Shane said, although the silence that remained seemed to add, *but not as good as Toby.*

"Hey—he's got one treed!" It was Toby, of course. The dog's hard bark had become a distant howl that echoed through the woods. "Grab a mule and let's get there before he tears the tree apart!"

Shane took off, sprinting into the woods. Vandardis swung onto the largest mule, Tom, which left me alone with Sass, whose withers came roughly to my navel. I threw a leg over the animal—and immediately fell off the other side. I tried again—and fell again. I heard Shane yell over his shoulder, "Behave, Sass!"

Sass wouldn't behave. He had a nasty trick of faking one direction, then turning another—then he'd eye me with supreme contempt as I landed—*thud*—on the ground. When I finally did get mounted, the animal began to plod south, back toward Ohio. I wanted to go west into the woods.

"Give him a whack!"

I'm not sure if it was Shane or Vandardis who was yelling advice, but I didn't hesitate to follow directions. I whacked . . . I whacked again . . . and Sass began to run; began to run with a vengeance . . . ran me deep into the woods, dodging trees that I couldn't see, under branches that I saw too late, bouncing me along as something inside my diaphragm made a ludicrous *ohoof-ohoof-ohoof* noise that refused to silence itself until a tree limb nearly decapitated me, then launched me butt first on the ground.

"See the 'coon?"

Yes. Yes, I saw it, for I had dismounted at precisely the right time. In the high limbs of a tree, frozen in the beam of Vandardis's light, were the golden eyes of a big raccoon. The animal didn't appear frightened. Indeed, the gleam in its eyes suggested that it was Sass the evil mule's soul mate.

"Good dog; good Toby!" Shane was congratulating his Night Champion. He had no way of knowing this, but his favorite dog would soon be killed by a car on a fast country highway under circumstances that would cause even Shane's father to weep like a child.

But that was a month away.

"Told you this was a wild sport!" Shane was talking to me as I peered up into the trees and the midwestern night beyond, seeing the wild limbs, autumn bare, and the far stars, although I was looking for a jetliner that would inevitably fly over—because I was thinking, You people don't know what you're missing. . . .

JUNGLE SURVIVAL SCHOOL

There are times when I would cheerfully stand in line to hear how it feels to be hit by a bushmaster, the largest and most venomous of the New World pit vipers, and there are times when I'm simply not in snakebite trim—say, just before ruck-humping it through dense rain forest at the army's Jungle Operations Training Center near Colón, Panama.

As I told instructor Staff Sergeant Elfren Padilla, "That's a fascinating scar, but I'd prefer to get the details later. Maybe sometime when we can both stand on cement. You ever get to Miami?"

But SSG Padilla, though he certainly doesn't flaunt his near-death encounter, felt it was a story I should hear. After all, I was about to join an Army National Guard platoon in heavy jungle where we would attempt one of the base's toughest training evolutions, the Mortar Employment and Maneuver course. On this all-day hell odyssey, courage was requisite, for the trials were garden variety: heat, mud, steep ascents, the certainty of ambush, water crossings, live mortar fire, killer bees, irritable monkeys, and, of course, snakes.

"Keep your eyes and ears open, you normally won't have any trouble," SSG Padilla told me. "But when it does happen, it happens quick. A little more than a year ago, I was walking up a jungle trail—you'll be doing a lot of that here. This base, it's mostly bush, sir. And wild."

I already knew that. The Jungle Operations Training Battalion (JOTB) headquarters, Fort Sherman, is located on a 23,000-acre wilderness reservation: volcanic rain forest, rivers, and mangroves at the Caribbean fringe of the Panama Canal Zone. No cities, no villages; nothing but jungle, swamp, and dark water.

"We've got a rule about animals here," SSG Padilla continued. "Look but don't disturb. Don't mess with the wildlife. It's their jungle, understand? So, I was walking up this trail all by myself, and I see a snake. Big snake, maybe seven, eight feet long, lying across the path. It's got diamond splotches on its back, so I figure it's a bushmaster. From our training, I know they get to be—what? twelve feet long?—and they sometimes travel in pairs. I don't want to get anywhere near this thing. So I cut into the jungle, way out around, then start uphill again. I take just a couple of steps, and all of a sudden there's this big snake's head coming at me—a blur. I threw my hands up to protect myself, and the next thing I know, I'm rolling backward down the hill, like I'd been shot. That's how hard the thing hit me. I fell maybe fifteen meters, then tried to keep on rolling because I figured the mate had gotten me and, by now, I didn't know where the other bushmaster was."

SSG Padilla held up his right hand: glossy, parallel scars ran to his wrist; the fang marks were nearly an inch apart. "I was wearing gloves, and the blood was just dripping out. I could feel the burn moving up my arm, so I wrapped a belt around it to slow the poison, found a stick to use as a crutch, then headed back down to link up with my patrol. By then, the pain was intense; unbearable. The jungle was moving—that's the way it seemed—everything getting blurry. I thought I was dead. But I didn't panic. That's what saved me. My training saved me."

SSG Padilla bushwhacked his way through a quarter mile of jungle. He doesn't remember how long it took. By the time he found his patrol, he was losing consciousness and nearly blind. Fortunately, there was a navy riverine boat nearby that rushed him to a helicopter, which then flew him to a hospital where Padilla spent the next several months recovering.

As Padilla's friend, Sergeant First Class Raul Rodriquez, told me, "It doesn't matter what your rank is, what kind of patches you got on your sleeves. Ranger, Airborne—that don't mean nothing to the jungle." We were standing near our Humvee transport on a road fringed by twelve-foot-high cuna grass. Nearby, a second battalion mortar platoon, 162nd Infantry, Oregon Army National Guard, off-loaded equipment: two dozen men in full battle gear and face paint, Kevlar helmets and weapons slung. Compared to this gung-ho apparition, venomous snakes seemed a mild threat— pristine distractions en route to dire objectives. Even so, Rodriquez gestured toward the cuna grass, which was our insertion screen, and the far emerald mountain beyond. "You go in there with a macho attitude, try to fight the jungle, it'll kick your butt every time. Nothing can stand up to it, man. You got to learn to move with it and stay out of its way. That's what this training's about. Because the only way to learn to survive is by surviving."

In that instant, survival became a pressing consideration. I heard a strange whistling sound that became an ascending scream as it grew nearer. *"Incoming!"*

There was an explosion, followed by another . . . then two or three more in quick succession: grenade and artillery simulators were being lobbed among us by an opposition force made up of Special Forces personnel.

"Bravo Company, move out! Move out!"

In the temporary chaos of concussion and smoke, the mortar platoon mustered in loose formation and sprinted off toward the cover of the cuna grass. I jogged along behind, leaving SFC Rodriquez to fall in with the invisible and fast-moving opposition force.

For the next eight hours, confronting a bushmaster would seem the least of my worries.

Since 1951, American and allied military personnel have been learning jungle survival skills at the Jungle Operations Training Center, just across Limon Bay from the old conquistador and pirate port of Colón. Over the years, emphasis evolved to include, then stress, the training of light infantry battalions in jungle combat operations. These days, the staff at Fort Sherman (18 officers and 115 enlisted men and women) spends twelve months a year hosting and training units from all military branches as well as non–Department of Defense personnel. As battalion commander Lieutenant Colonel J. C. Hiett told me, "We stay busy here. We teach thirty-three courses a year, including jungle warfare, aircrew survival, engineer jungle warfare, and opposing force orientation (for personnel who play the enemy in training exercises). Because we can provide full support facilities to visiting units, and because of our permanent staff, the training is not only inexpensive, it's the best jungle training in the world."

To learn survival skills in a jungle environment is a rare thing— and one reason I arranged with JOTB to participate in a course. But that was not the only reason. Personally, I was just as interested in the battalion's massive wilderness reservation that, since 1903, had been under U.S. control. How had the rain forest and its coastal fringe fared after decades of use by the military? It was something I wanted to see for myself.

I arrived during the second week of what is normally a three-week course and was immediately inserted into the training rotation of the visiting Oregon Army National Guard. The first couple of days consisted of core training events held at Fort Sherman, a beautiful old field battery of thick-walled offices and billets on grounds manicured like a tropical park. I spent a morning listening to Sergeant First Class Tom Kelley lecture on jungle plants and survival living ("None of you people are Dr. Doolittle, so you will not—repeat not—act like dumb shits and get close enough to talk to the goddamn animals!"), after which we were taken out onto the grounds to review which plants were edible, which were poisonous, which insects would bite the be-gezzus out of you, and which of the goddamn animals we were not to converse with. It was an invaluable introduction because viewing photos of flora and fauna is one thing, but examining living plants and animals anchors the memory electrodes.

There was a course on knots ("To tie a bowline, you *will* take the rope in your left hand and create a bight. . . ."), a course on small-boat handling ("You will *not* run your propeller over a fellow platoon member!"), and a review of jungle diseases ("Does the term *seriously fucked up* offend anyone here?") as well as a nonstop schedule of other courses. One of my favorites was Waterborne Insertion, part of which consisted of rolling out of a fast-moving boat into the tidal rip of the Chagres River. Another favorite was Mines and Booby Traps, taught by Staff Sergeant Faaaliga Matagi. SSG Matagi held class in the forest near an old battery fortification from which smoke boiled each time he detonated an explosion. Because SSG Matagi used the explosions to signal topic transitions, students inclined to doze didn't doze for long. As he pointed out, "This may be the most important course you take here! You kill a man, you eliminate one man from his unit. You wound a man with a mine or booby trap, you eliminate him plus the three or four men it takes to carry him out. Now, what do you think the enemy would rather do? Kill you or just blow off a part of you?"

A selfish love of lower extremities, plus the explosions, guaranteed that Matagi had our full attention.

After his lecture, the Samoan instructor invited us to hike a jungle course that had been booby-trapped—risky to the ego if not the body. But an Oregon National Guard lieutenant reassured me, saying, "Stick with me and we'll both get through this okay."

The lieutenant was half right. He detonated a simulator mine the instant he stepped on the path ("Aw, man, I'm dead!"). After I had made it through the trail, I accompanied the lieutenant back to where our equipment was stacked, only to see him blown up a second time: Matagi had booby-trapped some of the rucksacks. ("Shit, I'm dead again!")

After core training, the courses became more physical, and tougher. I rappelled off a forty-five-foot tower that was built to simulate a building exit and also a helicopter skid insertion. I accompanied a unit of Oregon National Guard engineers far up the Chagres River where, on a blocked tributary, they were tasked with blowing out some fallen trees. The engineers rigged more than half a dozen satchel charges, using blocks of C-4 plastic explosives. All went smoothly but for two things—the first of which I found most troubling. When the ten-minute time fuse was detonated, our boat stalled only a few yards from the explosives, and Sergeant Sarah O'Malley, of the JOTB staff, couldn't get the outboard started again. But she remained calm, checked the fuel line, reprimed the bulb, ignored the civilian sobbing at her side, and wheeled us out of the narrow creek with plenty of time to spare. The second glitch caused real trouble, though: the satchel charges didn't explode.

As Sergeant First Class David Conners, the JOTB engineer overseeing the operation, said, "The engineers from Oregon are going to be doing push-ups in the mud for this screwup! Now Sergeant Matagi and I have to go back in there, check the charges, rig a new fuse, and blow the thing. They're going to have one mad Samoan on their hands!"

Sergeants Conners and Matagi kindly invited me to accompany them, but, as I pointed out, if the worst happened, someone with reportage skills would be invaluable at the coroner's hearing.

Because the jungle warfare courses continue from first light until far into darkness, I didn't have a lot of free time. But I made use of the time I had. I got a topo map and savaged my rental car by driving the few mud roads that led inland. When the roads stopped, I got out and explored the military reservation on foot. Between Belize and Panama, I have been in a lot of wilderness areas, but I had never seen such massive untouched hectares of pristine rain forest: gigantic hardwoods blurring to the horizon, edged by the sea. There were no logging scars, no bulldozer tracks, no agrarian inroads or pasture splotches, the whole of which heralds the doom of rain forests worldwide. The 23,000-acre military reservation seemed a biological museum piece.

When I commented on this to the JOTB operations officer, Captain Jeff Grey, he said simply, "You can't have jungle training without jungle. The army takes very good care of this place."

But a more complex question was what would happen to the preserve (and an important training facility) when the Panamanian government assumed control on December 31, 1999?

It was a question for which the staff at Fort Sherman had no ready answer.

An ideal hike through primary rain forest would be the Mortar Employment and Maneuver course, if one wasn't sweat soaked, numb from exhaustion, and blinded by oxygen debt—which I was most of the time. And I wasn't even loaded down with weaponry, nor did I share the burden of carrying the heavy 81 mm mortar rounds the platoon was using. We threaded our way down slick ravines, waded creeks, hand-crawled up rooted promontories, some of us stopping only to retch in the greenhouse heat. The opposition force ambushed several times: eerie encounters not only because of the rifle chatter and surreal smoke detritus, but also because each skirmish reminded that this exercise was a pantomime of killing and dying; the lunatic ceremony of war in an environment that is itself slow war. Tropical rain forest neither welcomes nor resents. Its authority is the authority of unyielding processes—the crawling, skittering peat, leaf, and capillary grind of regeneration in which death is an apparition and shadow a weight. If I had to choose the habitat that I find most compelling, it would be a tough call between jungle or the saltwater littoral— ironic since both, through their indifference, make me vaguely uneasy. Sit too long on a decomposing log, and vines will soon constrict what insects have not carried away. Life is meaningless because life is all that matters. To enter either habitat is a kind of submergence; the chest expands as if affected by pressure, and the throb of one's own existence is absorbed by a silence that is more like darkness, the silence of the void. The jungle and the sea frighten me. There is no place I'd rather be.

Frankly, nothing I had learned from the JOTB instructors changed that. If anything, their lectures confirmed what I had long sensed: rain forest is a hostile environment; the slow war is real. What their instruction did do was make an irrational fear rational. They identified the dangers and they provided the techniques to circumvent them.

As Oregon Guardsman Major Dan Cameron told me, "To go into jungle hostilities without the kind of training we're getting here would be suicide."

One way or the other, it was true.

But this jungle warfare exercise *was* pantomime, so I actually enjoyed the rest that the ambushes afforded. The forest canopy wicked away the noise of grenades and automatic weapons, and I sat peacefully watching as morpho butterflies illuminated the gloom, fluttering by as if on a puppetteer's string. Once I saw a troop of capuchin monkeys swing past, perhaps intrigued by the noise. There were howler monkeys, too, though I never saw them. But I could hear them in the distance, their primate growls blending with the roar of live mortar fire.

It was a wild place; the kind of rare jungle where those not born to it must have training to survive.

If you ever get the chance, ask SSG Padilla. He'll tell you.

GATORMAN

I'm no admirer of tabloid newspapers, but last November, while standing in line at the grocery, I noticed a startling headline on the front page of the *Weekly World News:* "Half-Alligator, Half-Human Found in Florida Swamp!"

Was it possible that such a beast could have been captured without authorities notifying one of the nation's foremost authorities on kindred phenomena—me?

Yes. Apparently; although, even by the carrion standards of tabloid journalism, the claim seemed outrageous. But the accompanying photograph, at least, had to be given serious consideration. The image was terrible to behold: the dehydrated head and chest of a human growing from the body of some kind of *crocodi*. It had tiny little clawlike hands, and a facial expression that might be grotesque by decent standards but is all too common on Florida's beaches: the spring break glaze; a dumb, expectant look, as if the jaw has thawed too quickly beneath two frozen but eager eyeballs. Undeniably, the photograph had the ring of truth.

Even so, as an expert, my initial assessment was that an alligator had swallowed the bottom portion of some unfortunate man. A German tourist, perhaps—the Teutonic life expectancy in Florida is now exceeded by some species of mayfly. Indeed, a German tourist had recently disappeared a few miles from my own southwest Florida home. If a massive manhunt had not finally found him wandering crazed after three hellish nights lost in the mangroves, he, too, might have become part of the food chain, claimed by some bull gator that could not ingest more than half of anything weaned on sauerbraten. It made sense.

But the Weekly World News insisted upon another explanation. According to the accompanying story, the creature had been found, alive, by two hunters who wanted to kill it. Fortunately for the creature, a paleontologist, Dr. Simon Shute, happened to be working on a nearby Indian mound, and he, along with a Florida bureaucrat, interceded. After saving the creature, Dr. Shute and the bureaucrat, true to the traditions of their vocations, decided to take responsible action. The creature had presumably been living innocently in the Everglades, wild and free, a threat to no one. Their duty was clear: not only was this thing unregulated and unlegislated, worse, it was also untagged. So they roped the creature, caged it, then transported it to a secret marine lab in the Florida Keys.

"We are now conducting a search for more Gatormen," Dr. Shute was quoted as saying. "There are more out there."

Undoubtedly . . . if the story was true. And granted, some of the Weekly World News's details were compelling, if not convincing. But the whole tale was unraveled by a couple of key points that any sophisticated reader would spot as pure fantasy. One: if a Florida bureaucrat—or any bureaucrat—had truly been involved, he would not have attempted to capture Gatorman alone. He would have used his cellular phone to call for backup. Two: if Gatorman was accurately represented by the photograph, if his physiologic components had not somehow been reversed by a darkroom trick, the Weekly World News would not have quoted Dr.

Shute. They would have quoted the creature. Unless Gatorman spoke only German, in which case the tabloid would have invented a quote and used it anyway. Something tart and suitably Germanic, such as: "If I am to be extracted from this animal, let it be through the front exit!"

Obviously, the photograph was there, but the facts were not. It was a fascinating problem—not because I believed Gatorman existed, but because I have a long-standing interest in those strange and weird beasts that inhabit the human mind with far more certainty than they inhabit the regions that are credited with hiding them.

Intentionally or not, I think most outdoors people collect these stories; I have done so to the point of expertise. Indeed, they contribute to a pet theory of mine: the decline of a wilderness region can be gauged by the decline in the number of folklore creatures said to inhabit it. And another: folklore monsters instantly illustrate the geographical feature a region's human residents most fear.

Naturally, because I live in Florida, I was pleased to read about Gatorman—for the last few years, this state's most feared geographical feature has been Miami; its monster, the feral adolescents who stalk it. A half man, half alligator living in the swamps seemed pristine and reasonable in comparison. Just the rumor of such a thing earned back some respect for the Everglades. And it seemed to kick a little of the starch out of the bureaucrats who now dominate the place.

Over the next few months, I checked out details of the Gatorman story, and discovered the following:

- No paleontologist I could find had ever heard of Dr. Simon Shute.
- Shute's name does not appear in Florida motor vehicle records, nor in any Florida telephone directory.

- No one by the name of Dr. Simon Shute had ever applied for a state or federal grant—final, bedrock proof that the man did not exist.
- Edward Klontz, editor of the *Weekly World News*, might have a comment on the origin of the Gatorman story, but he doesn't return phone calls. (Not mine, anyway.)
- The *Weekly World News* is known as *Whacky World News* to some reporters at its sister paper, *The National Enquirer*, one of whom told me, "*Whacky World* is a big moneymaker, but you can't believe anything in it." (A searing indictment, considering the source.)

Yet the photograph was real, of that I was convinced. But each refuted detail was like a bullet in Gatorman's breast . . . or maybe his thorax. Hard to say for sure. Anyway, I dropped the investigation . . . until, by coincidence, a Louisiana friend mentioned that he knew a man who knew a man who, many, many years ago, had seen a creature fitting Gatorman's description, alive and on display, at a New Orleans brothel.

Am I making this up? Nope. Was my Louisiana friend? Nope. Was the long-gone man making it up? Probably.

It didn't matter. America and its wilderness are being urbanized, neuterized, and sanitized on an hourly basis, and those of us who love wild places—and the folklore creatures that are a measure of their vitality—have to be content with what we can get.

My search would continue. Even if it meant going to New Orleans.

Halloween's timing is off; spring is when the creatures come out. It's the first March thaw that lures to field and wood and bog the hibernants and winter dozers and God only knows what other hellish beasts. I don't say this from rumor or cheap hearsay; I know from early experience. I was just an infant when I had my first encounter with a yeti-like creature—or so my mother told me. We were living in a remote farmhouse in Ohio; my father, a highway patrolman, was away on duty when, one March night, my mother was awakened by the steady thud of someone—or something—walking outside. Then the house begin to shake, as if massive shoulders were being rubbed against the clapboard. For nearly an hour, the assault continued. We had no telephone. My mother lay awake until dawn, then went outside to investigate. There had been a fresh snow. Her description of what she saw never varied over thirty years: the prints of a barefoot man circled the house; each print was a broom handle and a half apart. Caught in the clapboard were tufts of silver hair. A farmer happened by, and the two of them measured the prints again. The farmer contacted the state patrol, but the snow melted, and the evidence disappeared.

In later years, I would say to her, "It was a cow." She would reply, "Honey, I know cows. I grew up with cows. Don't tell me about cows." I would say, "Then it was a bear." She would reply, "If it was a bear, I'd hate to try and buy shoes for it. The Sears catalogs don't mention size twenty D." Then she would add, in a mildly accusatory way, "And you slept through the whole blame thing."

What did she expect? I was an infant at the time, and not equal to a more mature response. When one is incapable of diving under the bed, one is better off sleeping. It's nature's way.

I believe what my mother said; I don't believe what she saw. Not the way she interpreted it, anyway. But the place where we lived was a desolate, unpeopled place—if not wild, at least isolated enough to empower all the potential of human imagination. That requires space. It requires inaccessible thickets, or swamps, or lakes without bottoms, or murky water, or a wooded place not veined with trails.

North Carolina, where most of my family has lived for genera-tions, had all of the above, plus plenty of aunts, uncles, and cousins to share tales about them. There were the Brown Mountain lights—lights of a ghostly source that we never saw, but we knew plenty of people who had. There was the Devil's Circle, where nothing ever grew, or could grow, because of an ancient curse. For a similar reason, there were the prints of a horse's hooves at Bath that were indestructible, and there was a creature that inhabited a bog on the PeeDee River, only some said it was a giant eel, and there was a pack of wild dogs that roamed the piney woods, grown huge from feeding on solitary fishermen and kids foolish enough to camp in the woods alone—which we often did. I grew up hearing all of this . . . but believing none of it (well, except for the one about those damn dogs). I wish I did. I wish I could.

Even so, I liked the stories. My theory about the relationship be-tween true wilderness and folklore monsters evolved. Which is why I am not surprised that, as the population grows and spreads, the regional creatures are disappearing. They are an endangered species not mentioned on any government list.

Before proceeding with my investigation into Gatorman, I de-cided to contact a few knowledgeable people around the nation and inquire into the well-being of creatures in other regions. I was lucky enough to reach Allan W. Eckert, author of the six-volume historical series *Narratives of America*. Eckert, from his home in Bellefontaine, Ohio, described in broad-brush fashion a variety of folklore monsters, including a gigantic black cat that was said to roam Ohio's hill country, and a great wolf of the Plains states that could destroy half a herd of cattle in a night. "I think most of these stories come from a period when people had enough leisure time to sit on their front porches and trade stories," Eckert told me. "Maybe that's one reason I seldom hear them now. When I did hear them, it was usually in the spring, when the weather allowed people to get out, peaking during the summer dog days, when the little newspapers didn't have much other news to publish."

In Nebraska, Joe Arterburn, as a member of Cabela's outfitters staff, converses daily with outdoors people, and I decided he would be a good one to ask. But, like Eckert, he hadn't heard a fresh story for many years. "You used to occasionally hear of a Big Foot sighting," Arterburn told me. "But not often. It stands to reason because there aren't a lot of places to hide in Nebraska."

I received a similarly disappointing report from writer Lionel Atwill in America's Northeast. "Even Champ, the monster of Lake Champlain, hasn't been reported in a while," he said. "The little town of Port Henry, New York, makes a living off those stories, and you'd think Champ would show a little more concern for their welfare."

The cynosure for reports of unidentified creatures, though, is the International Society of Cryptozoology, located in Tucson, Arizona. According to the society's secretary, J. Richard Greenwell, cryptozoology is different from other forms of the discipline in that it not only welcomes anecdotal information about undiscovered species, but also seeks it out. "A cryptozoologist becomes interested in a supposed animal based on previous information. Folklore, archaeological artifacts, native accounts, old historical narratives—we use all of these sources. Then we take a hard look at the data and try to decide if the supposed animal really could exist. If we're interested, we make a very deliberate search for the animal. It's a different philosophical approach than regular zoology."

The Cryptozoology Society is comprised of more than eight hundred members, according to Greenwell, many of them highly regarded professionals. "We're not in the sensationalism business," Greenwell told me. "Indeed, we avoid it. We try to go about the business of investigating previously unidentified species in a very careful way, and publish the results of field-workers in our quarterly journal. (An annual membership in the society is thirty dollars.) We try to assume nothing, then assign a percentage of probability. The Sasquatch, or yeti, for instance: if it does exist, I find it incredible that, despite hundreds of reported sightings from almost every state, not one specimen has been shot and killed by a hunter, or hit and killed on the highway, or collected in some fashion. Yet we still try to approach the possibility of it exisiting with an open mind."

Greenwell didn't think much of my folklore-requires-wilderness theory. "No, a whole new mythology has evolved," he said. "Urban folklore. It's like the stories of alligators and turtles living in the sewers of New York City. We've all heard the stories; some believe them. But there was only one verified case of a alligator being found in those sewers, and that was more than eighty years ago."

Nor did Greenwell give much credence to my story about Gatorman. "Years ago, there were a few reports about some kind of swamp creature that fits that description. But we've dismissed them as too bizarre. And the reports came from the Carolinas, not Florida."

My God. Was the bastard following me?

I went to New Orleans. I ate some great food; did the usual things. But I didn't find Gatorman. Over the phone, Angus Lind, a columnist for the *New Orleans Times-Picayune* told me a wonderful story about the loup-garou, a werewolflike creature said to live out in the bayou. Then I spoke with Joe Rau, a collector of antiques and stories, who said he knew a man who ran a small museum in Long Beach, Washington, who might have all the information I needed.

Rau was right—that's where I found the half man, half alligator as pictured in the *Weekly World News*. Not that I went to Washington. There was no need. Wellington Marsh, owner of Marsh's Free Museum in Long Beach, sent me a postcard of the creature—a creature he has owned, and had on display, for many years.

"I don't know how that newspaper got ahold of my postcard," Marsh told me, "and I don't know why they made up the story to go along with it. I call the thing Jake, and he's very popular with the folks who come through the museum. When they ask me about Jake, I tell them the truth. I don't know if he's real or not. But I know a man who knows a man who said he saw a creature just like Jake down someplace in Texas."

"Texas?"

"East Texas. In some kind of swamp or something. Not that I believe it."

Even so—the search continues!

SURVIVAL SPANISH

Despite my inability to speak a foreign language, I am convinced that, as a professional traveler, my cerebral powers have evolved beyond the norm. Indeed (and I say this objectively), my intellect has grown in direct proportion to the number of border guards I have bribed. Intellectually advantaged? I won't argue the point. It is precisely because of this process—"trekker's crazy wisdom" some call it—that I recently enjoyed a linear awakening regarding my own limits. I used to think I was too dumb to learn another language. Now I'm smart enough to know better. The reason I can't speak a second tongue is because I'm just too American.

It's true. All our qualities of greatness are balanced by this unfortunate reality: except for a few lucky immigrants, we are a multilanguageless people. It's not our fault; the butt-dumb factor plays no role—take my word for it. It is my own personal belief that, during the slow generational adaptive process, the chunk of American brain that controls foreign speech gradually withered to the size of a Muscat grape in autumn. Why? There are a couple of popular theories, all of which include garden-variety factors: bad vibes created by that idiotic Louisiana Purchase; the mass inhalation of flax during the Industrial Revolution; Prohibition; nuclear testing; acid rain; acid; those bastard aliens who (even though the government refuses to admit it) are beaming us up a piece at a time, then reassembling us, Tinkertoy fashion. . . .

I'm getting off the track. The truth is, most of us don't possess the circuitry to learn a foreign language. (The few Americans who do claim to be bilingual are probably lying. How would we *know*?) Does that mean we are doomed to spend our travel years communicating with pantomime and grotesque hand gestures?

Nope. Not anymore.

Recently, I attended a two-week Spanish course at Conversa, an intensive language school located a few miles outside San José, Costa Rica. It was at Conversa—where it rained all day every day—that I enjoyed my linear awakening. For eight days, I conjugated verbs until I got finger bloat. For eight days, I sat looking out that gloomy classroom window, trying to train my tongue to make foreign sounds. For eight days, I sat around meekly, feeling dumb as tire tracks, until I realized that, as an American, I had to attack Spanish with the same Spartan two-point philosophy I apply to packing for a trip: (1) survival isn't surviving unless it's fun; (2) take only what you need to survive.

After that, I was okay. I left the school, of course, and spent the remainder of my time traveling around Costa Rica, hiking the rain forests, dodging that country's noxious transit police, all the while compiling a list of Spanish phrases that we, the linguistically challenged, need in order to survive. During quiet evenings, I also drew on past personal experiences in places such as Nicaragua, Panama, and Cuba to add important phrases.

Is my behavior a condemnation of language schools? Not at all. If you are serious about learning a language, submersion is unquestionably the most efficient way to learn. But is it imperative that you take courses prior to roaming around Latin America? Not if you read the rest of this piece it's not.

What follows is, perhaps, the first genuinely practical guide to traveler's Spanish ever published. Let's be honest here: those idiotic language primers available in bookstores are worthless; worse, if we were to speak the inanities they teach, the locals would be well within their rights if they slapped us goofy just for being so dumb. "Will Hortensia watch television at her home on Wednesday?" Gad! What kind of boob would ask such a question? Since we don't know Hortensia, where and when she watches television is none of our concern (and, if we did know Hortensia, we probably wouldn't admit it). "Orlando is wearing new pants." Do you wonder why travelers sometimes die unexpectedly while touring Latin America? Authorities won't confirm it, but it is my personal suspicion that many of those deaths are directly related to fatuous non sequiturs such as this, most of them parroted from language primers. Avoid those books at all cost. They are not only useless, but also dangerous.

The Out There School of Survival Spanish, however, is both safe and effective. There's no need to learn the stock phrase "I don't speak Spanish," because they will know that you don't speak Spanish from the vacuous glow of your eyes. Give these people some credit. Something else you don't need to worry about is conjugating verbs. It's been my experience that Latin Americans are first-rate cryptologists, so don't be afraid to grab a verb and shoot from the hip. Same with nouns and adjectives that, for no good reason that I know of, indicate gender. But let's be reasonable: the person to whom you're speaking knows if he is a man or a woman, and he probably knows if you are a man or a woman, so what's the problem? Also, always keep in mind that, if you say something in Spanish, there's a real possibility that you will be answered in Spanish. So stay on your toes. (I've included a few common replies as examples.) Finally, because the countries of Central and South America suffer the same problems with con men and crime as the

United States, I've also included the kind of hardscrabble language you may need (or hear) in a tight spot.

Speaking to Airport Taxi Drivers

How much do you charge?
¿Cuanto cobra?

Let us negotiate a price *before* you take my luggage.
Negociamos el precio ANTES de que me lleva las maletas.

Your uncle's hotel sounds very nice, but I have reservations at the Holiday Inn.
El hotel de su tìo debe de ser muy lindo, pero tengo reservaciones en el Holiday Inn.

Please slow down.
Más despacio, por favor.

At high speeds, I get carsick.
A velocidades, me mareo.

This window doesn't work. May I break it?
La ventana no funciona. ¿Lo buedo romder?

Mother of God, pigs!
¡Madre de Dios, cerdos grande!

Yes, the crazy animal deserved to die. But must he ride beside me?
Sí, el bestia loco mereció morirse. ¿Pero es necesario que este sentado junto a mi?

I will change the tire, but don't expect a tip.
Cambiaré la llanta, pero no espere una propina.

At the Hotel Desk

I would like your least expensive room.
Quisiera su habitación menos cara.

I would like a better room.
Quisiera una habitación mejor.

Please explain the rope's function.
Por favor, expliqueme para que sirve la cuerda.

I would like any room not damaged during the recent earthquake.
Quisiera cualquier habitación que no sufrio daños en el temblor reciente.

The river is lovely, but I prefer a room with a shower.
El río is muy bonito, pero prefiero una habitación con baño.

Don't lie to me. I know the difference between a piranha and a carp.
¡No me mientes! Sé la diferencia entre una piraña y una carpa.

At Local Markets

I would like to change my American dollars.
Quisiera cambiar mis dólares Americanos.

Your currency is very pretty. Who's the guy with the top hat?
Soy dinero es muy bonito. ¿Quien es el hombre con la chistera de Monopoly?

No chicken hearts today, madam. Do you sell peanut butter?
No a los corazones de gallina hoy, señora. ¿Se vende crema de cacahuate?

The people of Taiwan are excellent craftsmen!
¡Le gente de Taiwan son artesanos excelentes!

No thanks. The sombrero impairs my vision.
No gracias. El sombrero bloquea la vista.

Will you throw in a couple of mangoes?
¿No puede dar de más un par de mangoes?

A Night on the Town

My compliments to the chef. The peccary is excellent!
Felicitaciones al cocinero. ¡El jabalí es riquísimo!

The rum is good, but I prefer the local beer.
¡El ron es bueno, pero prefiero la cerveza de aqui.

The local women do *what* to cause fermentation?
¿Las mujeres aqui hacen QUE para causar la fermentacion?

Keep those brewskies coming!
¡Sigua trallendo mas fermentarskies!

I don't question your abilities, but I am already married.
No dudo sus habilidades, pero estoy botin.

My friend is drunk and I am lost.
Mi amigo está borracho y estoy perdido.

My friend is lost and I am drunk.
Mi amigo está perdido y estoy borracho.

My apologies. I thought you asked me to dance.
Discúlpeme. Pense que me invito a bailar.

You have my full attention. Please stop kicking me.
Tiene mi atención completa. ¡Por favor, deje de patearme!

At Hospital

I am sick.
Estoy enfermo.

Relax! That is not gunfire, that is my stomach.
Calmese. No son balazos, es el estomago.

Everything was working fine when I left Miami.
Todo funcionaba bien cuando me salí de Miami.

If I break the pill in two, may I take it orally?
Si rompo la pildora en dos partes, puedo tomármela en la boca?

I prefer to believe that I was infected by a mosquito.
Prefiero creer que me infeccionó un mosquito.

Damn your oath! I've got things inside me that need to be killed!
¡Al demonio con su juramento! Tengo bichos adentro que necesitan ser muertos.

I was never asked to do that in the United States, and I am not going to do it here.
Yo no lo hize en los Estadoes Unidos, yo no lo voy hacerlo aqui.

If you've got the medicine, I've got the cash.
Si tiene la medicina, tengo el dinero en efectivo.

In a Tight Spot with Guerrillas, Thugs, or the Costa Rican Transit Police

Have I broken a law?
¿He violado un ley?

May I offer you a gift of money?
¿Puedo ofrecerle un regalito de dinero?

I love your uniform!
¡Me encanta su uniforme!

Your automatic weapons are so clean!
¡Sus ametralladoras son tan limpias!

Did I say American? I meant *Canadian*.
¿Dije Americano? Queria decir CANADIENSE.

Once again, those French bastards in Quebec have screwed up!
¡Otra vez, estos bueyes Franceses en Quebec han jodido todo!

You can have our women, but leave the plane tickets.
Pueden llevarse a nuestras mujeres, pero dejen nuestros boletos de avion.

My companion is out of money *and* estrogen. Hide your gun!
Mi compañera acabo plata Y el estrogeno. ¡Esconder su carabina!

Don't shoot! We are musicians!
¡No disparar! ¡Somos estrellas de Beatles!

At Border Crossings/Customs/In Jail

(Note: As mentioned, there is a very real danger that, if you speak in Spanish, you will be answered in Spanish. Key words and phrases for which you need to be alert include: ¡Mierda loca!; ¡Disparar ahora!; ¡Arreste los gringoes! Don't worry about translations. When the big crunch comes, the less you know the better. It's like dealing with a bear: play dumb. But if you hear any combination of the above, let panic be your guide.)

Yes, I have a receipt.
Sí. Yo tengo recibo.

I have a prescription for that.
Yo tengo prescripción. ¡Sincero!

Did I say twenty dollars? I meant *fifty*.
¿Dije veinte dólares? ¡Queria decir CINCUENTA!

I have a powerful friend at the American embassy.
Yo tengo una amigo importante en la embajada de Americano.

Assassinated? Then my work is done here. The capitalist pig deserved to die.
¿Asesinato? ¡Bueno! ¡Bueno! El puerco capitalista mereco muerto.

Oh, you meant *rooster* fighting? Sorry. I was just trying to follow orders.
¡Oy, oy, oy! ¿Lucho de gallos? Discúlpeme. Yo soy estupido, no perverso.

Nice jail you got. Much better than my hotel room.
El cárcel is magnifico. Mucho mas bueno mi hotel.

NORIEGA SAT HERE

Because the Panama Canal will be officially transferred to its host republic at noon on December 31, 1999, and because for the first time in eighty-five years one of this century's greatest engineering achievements will no longer be under U.S. control, the country has lately been caught up in a frenzy of transitional activity, from coast to Panamanian coast. But to the Americans I met during a recent tour of the Zone, there was no business more pressing than the matter at hand: to steal back Manuel Noriega's fabled bar stools.

"Bar stools?" I asked Tom Pattison.

"Yeah, three of them," he replied. "Nice ones, too, made out of really good wood. I helped liberate them from Noriega's private island in 1990, just after the U.S. invasion to capture the *generalisimo*—Operation Just Cause. And then some bastard stole them from me. If there's one thing we Zonies can't tolerate, it's a thief."

T-Bird, as Tom Pattison is known, is the consummate Zonie, part of that tight, die-hard enclave of Americans who have helped keep the canal operating as smoothly as a Swiss clock for the better part of a century. A strapping guy who looks vaguely like Jethro Bodine, he's a third-generation resident of the ten-mile-wide, forty-three-mile-long anachronism that until 1979 was the Panama Canal Zone.

We were sitting outside at the Balboa Yacht Club, southwest of Panama City, only five hundred yards off the Pacific channel that leads from the canal locks at Miraflores. There were interesting vessels passing by: cargo ships, stadium-size cruise liners, an American nuclear submarine. The Balboa Yacht Club was once a classy way station of international travel as well as a polestar of Canal Zone society, but the place has fallen into disrepair. It now looks like an abandoned warehouse, its windows either boarded up or smashed. The formal restaurant upstairs was closed years ago. The steps are wobbly, the flush toilets tricky. Yet it's still a tradition among Zonies to meet on the downstairs deck at dusk, because the Balboa Yacht Club is one of the planet's truly blessed spots to watch a sunset.

That's what T-Bird and I were doing as we sat beneath ceiling fans in the bar, looking out over the segment of water that since 1914 has joined the Pacific and the Atlantic as inexorably as it has united three generations of a unique American strain. It's a strain soon to become extinct. Twenty years ago, there were more than 10,000 Americans working on the canal. Today, there are fewer than 600. This steady downsizing is all the result of the Panama Canal Treaty, a sweeping document signed by President Jimmy Carter back in 1977. When the treaty went into effect two years later, the U.S.-run Panama Canal Company was abolished. That meant no more Zone legal system, no more Zone police or fire departments, no more Zone schools. Since then American workers have been "involuntarily retired" at a steady clip, and the gradual transfer of power has proceeded exactly according to plan. In December 1999, the final transitional step will be made: the canal itself will be turned over to Panama and to the Panamanian staff that will run it in toto. "I may have to leave here in two years," T-Bird said. "We may all have to leave, eventually."

But T-Bird wasn't leaving, he said, without his stools. He went on to explain their odd, sordid history: as the smoke was clearing from the U.S. invasion of Panama, T-Bird and a couple of Navy SEALs decided to go diving for spiny lobsters off Naos, a small island connected by causeway to the Panama City suburb of Balboa. Naos had been one of Noriega's infamous lairs, and he'd declared it off-limits to the general populace. "So no one had been diving around Naos for years," T-Bird said. "My friends and I figured it would be loaded with lobsters, and we wanted to be the first ones there after the invasion."

According to T-Bird, the SEALs took an immediate interest in a certain octagonal house on the island that locals knew as Manny's Hideaway. It was rumored to be Noriega's party retreat, a place with reflective glass windows behind which, it was said, many strange and depraved acts had been performed.

"While I was out there diving for lobsters, the SEALs broke into the house, no problem, and decided to take a few choice souvenirs from Noriega's bar. All of a sudden, furniture was raining down on me, big leather-back swivel stools dropping through the water like depth charges! Normal people would have tossed them into the boat, but not those guys. With them, everything's got to get wet first." T-Bird somehow made it home with three of the stools, his share of the spoils of war. Then one day in 1992, he returned home to discover that he'd been burgled. Since only the stools were stolen, T-Bird surmised that whoever took them had to have been someone who'd heard about their unusual history.

But now he'd hatched a plan. He wanted me and my traveling companion, an Iowa-born resident of Balboa named Jay Sieleman, to go on a kind of treasure hunt. "The other Zonies, they're not going to tell me where my stools are," T-Bird said. "To them, it's all just a big joke, like a game of keep-away. But if you get Sieleman to take you all around the Zone, well, they might tell you the real story." It was an attractive proposition—a built-in excuse to get out of Panama City and sample the mood of the last remaining Americans. Certainly Sieleman, an old lawyer friend of mine who's now assistant general counsel for the Panama Canal Commission, could give me a pretty good entrée into Zonie society. And if I got lucky and found T-Bird's stools, there was a real possibility I could shame him into offering me one of the things out of gratitude. A war relic from the hideaway of Generalísimo Manuel Noriega would be a first-rate keepsake.

T-Bird wished me luck and impressed upon me the mission's importance. "I risked too much to get those damn things," he said. "Dealing with the Panamanian Defense Forces? Man, I could've been killed! By God, I'm taking those stools with me."

"Let's get started off on the right foot," Sieleman told me. "I hereby decline to listen to or even acknowledge anything you might say concerning bar stools that were allegedly misappropriated by—or stolen from—that coconut-head, Tom Pattison. I don't know what happened, and I refuse to learn. Over the last decade, our friend T-Bird has been heading for a fall, but it's only now that he's truly begun to debauch himself. I've got my reputation to consider."

As he said this, Sieleman was at the wheel of his minivan, and we were driving northwest along the canal, passing through sweltering suburbs. He waited patiently while I watched in amazement as a Japanese freighter was lowered through the locks at Miraflores. After that, we made a stop at Lakeview Golf Club, a long-established West Indian stronghold, where we ate pig's feet and watched a cricket match. Clearly, as far as Sieleman was concerned, he'd signed on for an innocent tour of the region. Any discussion of stolen goods would not be tolerated.

Sieleman is a laid-back American in his midforties with a finely tuned sense of lawyerly style: he's got immaculate hair; his clothes hang just right. Since moving to Panama in 1987, he's also become a passionate mountain biker and rain forest devotee. Among his numerous enthusiasms, Sieleman is probably the most important promoter and dedicated patron of blues in the region—which is why he spends so much time in bars "doing research." His house is a shrine to his favorite blues musician, Taj Mahal. Or so he'd told me. "You've got to see my place when we get back," Sieleman insisted. "You'll love it!"

No doubt I would. Back in the late 1910s and 1920s, the Panama Canal Company had built classic lapstrake homes of a military style known as "U.S. Billets, Tropical." Constructed on stilts and made of California redwood (specially freighted in for the job), with roofs of copper sheeting, they're open and airy but as solid as a seagoing ship. They were built for the long haul at a time when carpenters took their craft seriously. As we pulled into the village of Gamboa, about midway between Panama City and Colón, the old homes were a reminder of just exactly what it was the Zonies were giving up: orderly streets of trim white houses set beneath tropical green, with porches that looked out over a broad stretch of the canal. Since 1979, Gamboa has seen a gradual influx of Panamanians, but overall the village still resembled some American small town from the 1950s that had been picked up, public swimming pool and all, and transported to the rain forest. Earlier, Richard Wainio, a child of the Zone who is now director of the Panama Canal Commission's Office of Executive Planning, had explained to me the original thinking behind these neighborhoods. "During the old days," he'd said, "the Zone worked on the company town concept. Housing, schools, parks, movie theaters—everything was provided. The company wanted to attract stable, career-oriented family people and keep them happy here not just for a few years, but for their entire lives."

If their domestic life was cozy, the work assignment the Zonies faced was daunting as hell: to endure intense heat, insects, and tropical diseases while hacking their way through forty miles of jungle; to construct one of the largest earth dams ever built while devising an enormously complicated system of locks; to keep ship traffic moving despite depressions and wars and political unrest—and to keep doing it 365 days a year for more than six decades without a single strike, walkout, major screwup, or scandal.

Just as the company had hoped, many stayed on for the rest of their lives. Which is why the transition is now proving to be so traumatic for the last remaining hangers-on. It's been a wholesale uprooting that Sieleman, a more recent transplant, has found difficult to watch. "As a good liberal Democrat, I'm for the treaty," he told me, "but it's worth noting what the treaty did to the people all these houses were built for. As of '79, the sons and daughters of Zonies have found it harder and harder to become permanent employees of the commission. The treaty took a lot of jobs away, and it changed a lot of futures. It doesn't mean there shouldn't be a treaty—there should. But it sure affected a lot of people."

People, for instance, like Bob Dollar, the chief engineer of the tugboat *Gamboa*. A can-do guy in his late forties with a ponytail and tattoos reflective of his Harley past, Dollar grew up a Zonie and will be leaving, like most of the others, in 1999. One afternoon we were out on the *Gamboa*, and Dollar's skipper, Oliver Beckles, allowed me to steer the ninety-four-foot, 258-ton tug southeast for a stretch of the canal. Below, in the galley, chicken and rice were simmering on the stove, adding texture to the pleasant maritime odors of diesel, electronics ozone, and polished brass and teak. Off to our right, the shoreline was a vine-veil of tropical foliage. To our left were rolling green hills, steamy countryside that seemed somehow aloof from the canal's steady ply of commerce.

It was nice being out on the tug, but also nerve-racking. I had to pass by a couple of Japanese freighters port to port, a tricky maneuver in tight quarters. Any lapse of judgment might instantly result in a couple million dollars' worth of damage. Those few white-knuckle minutes pressed home for me the operative reality: that down inside the canal's narrow confines, it's all business. Bob Dollar works at the same job that his late father worked before him. "Sometimes," Dollar said, "when I'm on a different vessel, I'll go through the ship's log, and there's my dad's name. Chief engineer, same as me. I get a kick out of that. It means something knowing that my family played a small part in the history here."

Dollar began to describe what will probably be his final project in the Zone. "Over the last few years," he said, "our duty has been to handle the dredges and scows that are widening Gaillard Cut, one of the narrowest parts of the canal. By the time we're done, though, it'll be wide enough to handle two-way traffic. It's always been kind of a bottleneck." Then he added, "I don't want to sound like a dweeb, but I like the idea that when we turn the canal over, it'll be bigger and better than it's ever been. After that, it's up to the Panamanians."

Dollar, who plans to move to St. Croix in 2000, said he wasn't bitter about the prospect of leaving. "All I'm trying to do is concentrate on enjoying these last couple of years," he said. "I think all the Zonies are. It's a good place. We all know what we're losing. We'll miss it terribly, but that's the way things go. It makes me pay attention to things, knowing I'll be the last American here to do what I do."

While in Gamboa, I was invited to three different parties, where I was afforded ample opportunities to make discreet inquiries about T-Bird's bar stools—but no one seemed to have a clue. At one of these parties, however, I did receive an intriguing anonymous note: "Have you searched T-Bird closely?" it said. "The stools may have disappeared while he was sitting on them."

Yes, very cryptic. Clearly the Zonies, so long marooned from the world, were experts at manufacturing entertainment. Less obscure was their penchant for reminiscing. I filled my notebook with snatches of rueful conversation and many drunken declaratives that seemed to distill life in the Zone. The Zonies sometimes spoke as though they'd already left the place: "The best part of living here was surfing at Pina Beach, waterskiing near the docks in Gatun Lake, Friday night dances at the Red Barn in Margarita, sneaking caimans into the Gamboa swimming pool. . . ."

"There was a big-time rivalry between Cristobal High School [on the Caribbean] and Balboa High [on the Pacific]. Didn't matter what clique you were in—jocks, straights, juicers, stoners—everyone got on the TransIsthmian train and partied all the way to the football game."

"When you think about it, Zonie life was just about as good as it gets. No unemployment, almost no crime, first-rate housing, great facilities, great security. But man, if someone screwed up bad, the company would ship those people back to the States just like that! One day the family would be there, the next day they'd be gone."

In the old days, a favorite pastime was to sit on porches, eating chorizo sausages, drinking Soberana beer, and playing a game that was actually first dreamed up by T-Bird. The game was "You Know You're a Zonie If . . ." From my notebook: "You know you're a Zonie if you are intimidated by the menu choices at a U.S. Pizza Hut. If the primary color of your car is gray putty Bondo. If your lifetime goal is to own a fireworks stand. If your boat has a better paint job than your house. If you consider a six-pack and a bug zapper quality entertainment." And finally: "You know you're a Zonie if you can name the president who gave away the canal, but you can't name any since."

This same sort of playfully combative nostalgia was equally in evidence among the Americans I met in the Atlantic gateway town of Colón, about twenty-five miles north of Gamboa. A city of 156,000 people, Colón is still a favorite destination of drunken sailors. It's a place of ratty bars, prostitute curb stations, and way too much traffic on busted streets that were never designed to handle the burden of what Colón has become—Central America's busiest and tackiest duty-free seaport. My first stop was the Elks Lodge, BPOE 1542, where I made a courtesy call on Camille Mazzerolle, exalted ruler of the lodge. Mazz, as everyone knows him, has worked in the Zone off and on since 1955, and he is a social fixture among the Zonies. Though Mazz clearly hated to see the place change, he said he thought the transition was going as smoothly as could be expected. "The Panamanians are good people," he said. "They'll do their best. But I'll tell you what, we Zonies are going to throw one hell of a good-bye party on December 31, 1999. And we're going to have a party every year after that at our annual reunion in Orlando."

Later that day, I met a couple of Canal Commission employees (requesting anonymity) who saw a much bleaker future for the canal. Look what happened, they said, when the Panamanian government took control of the TransIsthmian train. Throughout all the decades of Zone operation, they said, it had been a dependable means of daily transportation between Panama City and Colón. Now, they claimed, the entire rail system was a wreck. The train was in such bad shape that it seldom ran more than once or twice every couple of weeks, and there was no dependable schedule. "The Panamanians can't handle it," one of my companions contended. "It's going to be an absolute mess when they take over the canal."

Back in Panama City, though, my Zonie friends quickly buoyed my spirits. "You worry too much," T-Bird told me. "No matter what happens, you can't help but love this place."

When I visited Sieleman's classic old digs in Balboa for the first time, he was equally upbeat. He said, "The Panamanian National Assembly is doing everything it needs to do to make certain that all the legal infrastructure is in place when the transfer takes place. You don't think they know the world is watching?" As he spoke, I was roaming around his living room, looking at all the *Rolling Stone* covers and the man's collection of beer bottles, listening to the Taj Mahal CD he had playing on his elaborate sound system.

"Grab a seat," he said, "and relax. We'll have a Soberana, then head down to the yacht club for sunset." So I grabbed myself a seat—a heavy, high-back bar stool, one of three in Sieleman's kitchen. They were nice ones, too.

THE JUMPER'S CLUB

Some years ago, my friend Bobby Fizer jumped out of a speeding boat at night and without warning into a moonless, saltwater bay—outrageous behavior that I normally would have applauded had it not been my boat, my liability insurance, and my Coast Guard captain's license that were on the line.

Authorities get testy when it comes to losing passengers.

One moment Bobby was at my side, then I felt the boat list heavily to starboard, and the next moment he was gone.

Confused, I yanked back on the throttle as I yelled to one of our companions, "Hey—where's Fizer?" Professional that I was, I knew that it was unlikely to misplace a former Ohio State linebacker on an eighteen-foot skiff.

"He jumped. The idiot just jumped."

"He *what*?" I was already wheeling the boat around. "You mean he *fell* overboard?"

"Nope." Our companion—his name was Hervey—said it again: "The dope jumped."

Gad! We'd been doing thirty-five miles an hour at the time.

Hervey said, "It was his idea. Leave him. He'll make it back."

We were two, maybe three miles from the mainland. "I'm not even sure he can swim."

"He can swim. He's from Ohio, isn't he? Almost everybody from Ohio can swim."

Behind us, the demarcation of sea and sky was a rind of January gray. The bay was black and without borders. I had a small flashlight, but its beam was no match for a winter night with clouds.

I panned the light around. Nothing. When I switched if off, Hervey was quiet for a moment, then he said, "There he is. You see him?"

No, I didn't see Fizer. What I did see was a rhythmic, boiling green light in the distance. Earlier, we had remarked on the quantity and brightness of phosphorescence in the water. Created by bioluminescent flagellates that fire up like lightning bugs when disturbed, our boat wake had been an expanding cone that flamed like turquoise paint. There were only a few weeks in each year—always on the dark of the moon—when the phosphorescence was so vivid.

I said, "Yeah, anything that size, it's either Bobby or a small whale."

Hervey refused to lend credence to sarcasm. "I sure hope so. I've never seen a whale before."

Approaching a swimming Fizer by boat was like seeing some monster from a 1950s horror movie who had been illuminated internally by a radiation experiment. His hair was glowing, so were his face and his hands. When we were near enough, I switched off the engine, and I listened to him yell, "What a hoot! Watch this—" And he began to do a clumsy synchronized swimming routine in which each sweep of his hands created contrails as bright as a comet's tail. "I had to do it," he explained as he climbed back aboard. "That stuff hypnotized me. I kept imagining what it would be like to jump—you know, just let go and bail. It was even better than I thought. It was like jumping into the *stars*, man."

Fizer was a favorite traveling companion of mine. On the road, all partnerships are a balancing act, and Fizer was ideally unbalanced. He was very funny but was also prone to dangerous behavior—producing firearms at inappropriate times and in unexpected places was not out of character. Fizer was almost always late or never arrived, but he was a gifted athlete and a good guy to be with in a tight spot. Sappy greeting cards aside, a partnership is defined, not measured, by one's willingness to go to the aid of another. It is an obligation that blends conscience and accountability, and in that way Fizer was always dependable.

Another way that he was dependable—and another reason he was a good traveling companion—was that he was continually inventing bizarre and outrageous things to do. The Dead Writers Wiffle Ball World Series was one. The Three-Mile Golf Classic (literally) was another. Now, with this unexpected leap, he was blazing a new trail. The question was: would we follow?

"It's one of the most awesome things I've tried," he told us. "It's like you're flying through space, then there's this explosion of light. You tumble through it like you're a meteor or something." Another component, Fizer noted, was all the big sharks that cruised the area. "It adds just the right *edge* to the whole deal," he said. "Just waiting for the boat to find me was a rush. You know the kind of tension I'm talking about?"

The guy was almost unfairly persuasive. That evening, the Jumping-Out-of-the-Boat-at-Night-Club was founded. I'm not going to sit here and romanticize an activity that is adolescent and dangerous. Indeed, I'll be blunt: don't try it. Do not sneak to the stern and jump from a vessel that is traveling thirty or forty miles an hour over black water. Don't let anyone you know try it. It's not worth the risk.

Still . . . it is a stunning thing to feel one's boat heel unexpectedly, then to look back and see a volcanic eruption as one's passenger smacks the water. It is even more stunning to launch oneself into darkness, then to be swallowed up by an exploding nebula of star-streaks and swirls.

The Jumper's Club enjoyed a vogue of three or four years—always on moonless nights when the phosphorescence was bright. The membership was small, select, and included people who are now administrators and teachers, plus a National Book Award winner and the manager of a major league baseball team. Fizer's contagious madness was no respecter of intellect. But at a certain point in the maturing process we all realized how stupid it was, and we closed the books on the membership and the club. The increasingly blasé attitude of fellow members was also a factor. It got to the point where, when one jumped, one couldn't be certain the person driving the boat would return in less than an hour—or return at all.

"It's getting harder and harder to maintain that edge," Fizer explained one night as we approached my rickety dock. "I mean, it's still a hoot, but after twenty or thirty times, it's just not . . . spontaneous anymore."

A few weeks ago, Bobby Fizer returned to that same rickety dock for a small ceremony that we were holding in his honor. He was uncharacteristically punctual, but only because he came with his brother, Scott, a man of fraternal sensibilities and bulk—which is to say bear-size. With them was their father, their stepmother, their sister, Tanya, and Bobby's two daughters. When Scott saw me, he approached quickly and removed the lid from a small container. "You won't believe what I just did," he said. "I tripped coming across the road and spilled some."

He was talking about the urn he was carrying. He was talking about what was inside.

I told him, "The guy liked roads. Don't worry about it."

Scott was sifting the contents of the urn through his fingers. "Look at this stuff, it looks like cat litter. The whole package, it weighs like fifteen pounds. When he was in pretty good shape, he weighed what? Two-thirty? I can't believe it. I still can't believe it. We've got that much water in us?"

He was talking about the way his brother had been; the way he was now. He was talking about Bobby, who had died of natural causes at the age of forty-two.

A friend told me recently that you know you've reached middle age when your travel partners start dying.

"*Natural causes* is the key phrase," he said. "Listen for that, and you'll know."

He was right. It is January, the month for review, and I hereby openly and freely admit that I now qualify. I am officially middle-aged. This is less an admission than it is an offering. In recent years, many of our kindred have pierced the generational barrier, and those suffering its distress should take heart—most of us will continue to age despite the fact that we are already plenty old enough, and the bullheaded among us will keep right on traveling.

Still, the phrase *natural causes* is unsettling. I think my friend was referring to any contributor that did not include foreign taxis, air crashes, faulty climbing gear, boating accidents, and acts of God or street bandits. In short, he was excluding events in which we have a hand in the decision-making process. If there is risk in what we do—and there is always risk—then we have the option of throttling back and living safe but boring lives, or we have the option of embracing those risks and trying to manage them as best we can. Perhaps that is why the phrase *natural causes* is so disturbing. It describes a process over which we have no authority and less control. It transforms death from an external variable into an internal eventuality in which our own bodies turn traitor. To accept that is the challenge of middle age and, to my way of thinking, requires a spunky screw-it-all attitude and the same kind of emotional untethering that travel itself requires.

There's a lot to be said for just letting go. It also helps to keep in mind that that bastard grim reaper is loose in the room, and moving targets are harder to hit.

All of my friends, all of the people I most admire, are movers. Bobby was a mover; so was my buddy Totch Brown.

Totch was born in the mangrove backwaters of the Everglades. His father was a Cracker entrepreneur. His father fished, made moonshine whiskey, and smuggled rum for a living. Totch carried the family legacy into modern times by fishing and smuggling in illegal flora from Central America. "Pot hauling," Totch called it. Because Totch was a brilliant waterman, the Coast Guard never caught him. Because Totch wasn't a brilliant bookkeeper, the IRS did.

Not long after Totch was released from a federal penitentiary, he offered to accompany me to Panama. "Randy," he promised, "there are men in Panama who will do anything I tell them to do. I've made some investments in those parts."

Totch had a strong artistic side. He wrote country music and published one very good book. He was a brilliant storyteller and not averse to hyperbole. I asked Totch to accompany me not just because he was a favorite travel partner, but also because I wanted to find out if he was exaggerating his familiarity with Central America.

He wasn't. Totch's personal driver picked us up at the international airport in Panama City. Totch seemed to know just about everyone, and everyone seemed delighted to see Totch again. As we were being driven to the Continental Hotel on Via Espanã Avenue, Totch would occasionally nudge me, point to a building, and say, "See that place? I used to own me a business in that place." He was showing off a little, letting me know that he once had money and the wisdom to make it work for him. He'd point again and say, "That building across the street? I used to own me a business there, too."

Asking Totch what business he'd been in was a precarious matter with potential legal ramifications, but I asked anyway. His answer surprised me.

"What I did in Panama City, Randy, was open me a string of seven tanning parlors."

Tanning parlors? As delicately as I could, I pointed out that tanning parlors seemed a risky investment in a city that lies near the equator and that is populated with people who are pretty dark to begin with.

Totch thought about that for a moment. "By God, I wish I'd talked to you before I done it," he said. "Every one of them bastards went bust. I lost a bundle."

Later, I realized that Totch may have used the word *tanning* as it relates to the curing of animal hides. But if he meant it that way, he was gentleman enough not to make me feel stupid by explaining—a great quality in a travel companion.

Another friend who possessed great qualities and kept moving was Ginny Clements. Ginny was the stepdaughter of Mack Hamby, one of my favorite people in the world—and not just because he managed the marina at which I was a fishing guide for thirteen years. When Ginny was in high school, she liked to canoe through the mangrove estuaries, and she also loved getting out on open water. Ginny was a good person to be with in a boat. Having grown up on the marina property, she knew how to handle herself.

As big and pretty and strong as she was, Ginny had health problems early on. She was told it would be difficult to have children, but Ginny married my buddy Nick, who worked at the marina, and they went ahead and had a boy and a girl anyway.

"I don't have time for experts," she told me once. "If they know so much, why are they so easy to prove wrong?"

Nick and the children liked to travel as much as Ginny did. They had boats, all kinds of boats, and they took car trips, too. They were, in fact, staying at a cabin in the North Carolina mountains when Ginny realized that she was sick again.

"Can you believe it?" Nick would ask me on nights when I stopped by to help with Ginny and the kids. "I still can't believe it."

It is the rhetorical question most commonly asked when the body of a loved one turns traitor.

Ginny died in the winter. Totch hit the high trail in May. Natural causes, both—though in light of our predicament, and in terms of the adventure in which we are engaged, all causes seem no less natural than, say, leaping off a speeding boat into black water.

I didn't tell Scott or his family, but Bobby's funeral was my third within a few months, the main difference being that I was asked to give the eulogy—an honor that is impossible to covet and harder to dodge.

I can't remember exactly what I said to that crowded room. I know I said, "The guy was a hoot. Wasn't he a hoot?" because that was a favorite expression of his. I know I also talked about returning from Mariel Harbor, Cuba, to Key West during the 1980 refugee boatlift. Some friends and I had spent a lot longer in Mariel than we expected, and we had returned with a lot more refugees than we had wanted. Now stranded in Key West, filthy, soaked, and without much money, we discussed who among our friends we could call and ask to drive six hours, pay the tab for our cheap motel, then turn around and drive us six hours home again.

We called Bobby, who yelled, "Are you nuts? Do you think I'm crazy?" But he agreed, of course, and we set about spreading our things out to dry while we slept.

At some time after 3 A.M. I was awakened by a massive banging noise, then the door was kicked wide open, and there stood Fizer filling the doorway. He looked gigantic and deranged in his cowboy hat, boots, and mirrored shades; probably *was* deranged, judging from the half-empty bottle of Wild Turkey whiskey in his hand. He tilted his shades up just enough to see, then he surveyed our wreck of a room before he spoke for the first time. "You people are a menace to yourselves and everyone who knows you," he said. "If the cops show up, I'm going to claim I've placed you all under citizen's arrest. I've got a gun; I can do it." He touched the rim of his cowboy hat—a Clint Eastwood gesture. "Just so you maroons know where I stand."

I told that story at the eulogy, and I said something else because I thought it might make the man's family feel better. I told them, "Bobby had great energy, and energy cannot be destroyed. It has nothing to do with religion or hope. It is a fact of physics."

But standing on my rickety dock with Fizer's family, I wasn't so certain that I believed it was true. Middle age does not suffer wistful platitudes gladly. So I listened to the family speak, and I tried to comfort the daughters as best I could before boarding my skiff with Scott, his sister, and his father to spread the remainder of Bobby's ashes in the bay. It was nearing dusk, but it was not a pretty day. There was wind and clouds. The family had been hoping for a symbolic sunset. Instead, they got rain, then more rain.

Scott, with his fraternal sensibilities, was not pleased. He sat to my right, the urn in his lap, glowering at the sky as we powered off toward a place in the bay that was one of Bobby's favorite spots.

"I hate rain," he growled. "You know why I hate rain?"

Yes—because he plays semipro football. He's a defensive back and placekicker, and all placekickers hate rain.

"Damn right," he said. "I *despise* the stuff."

Spirits were no higher in the forward part of my boat, and in an attempt to lighten the mood I pointed ahead to a section of deep water and began to tell them about our Jumping-Out-of-the-Boat-Club.

"This is where we did it," I told them. "Always right in here and usually going about this fast."

"At night?" Tanya, the sister, said. "You guys were nuts. What a hoot."

The father, Robert Sr., smiled a little. "That sounds like him. That sounds just like him. He loved stuff like that."

Scott said, "Yeah, he was such a maroon," then was silent for a moment, looking at the blur of water. I didn't expect Scott to do what he did next, although I highly approved. What he did was nudge me, flash a wicked grin . . . then he flung the urn overboard. It was the first time I'd heard him laugh in several days when he called, "Hey, Dad, guess what—Bobby just bailed."

I circled back, switched off the engine, and we drifted through the blooming, moving turbidity created by the ashes; a slow cloud of reds and grays that, on a day so dark, seemed as lucent as starlight. . . .

THE LOST DIVERS

On Sunday, November 6, 1994, a Jayhawk H-60 Coast Guard helicopter was operating fifty-two nautical miles off the west coast of Florida when a crewman spotted a naked man on the highest platform of a 160-foot light tower. The man was waving what appeared to be a wet suit. He was trying to attract the helicopter crew's attention.

The helicopter was in the area searching for a twenty-five-foot pleasure boat that had been reported overdue. According to the report, the vessel *Sea Esta* had left Marco Island the previous Friday morning with a party of four Canadian men. The men had planned to spend the day offshore, fishing and SCUBA diving, but had not returned Friday afternoon as expected. The Coast Guard had been searching for *Sea Esta* since Friday night. The crew of the Jayhawk had been looking for a disabled boat, not a man waving a wet suit from a light tower.

The helicopter flew east past the tower, banked south, then hovered beside the platform. One of the crew signaled the man with a thumbs-up—it was a question. The man signaled a thumbs-up in return—he was okay. Then the man pulled on his wet suit, climbed down to a lower platform, and dove into the water. The crew of the Jayhawk dropped a basket seat and winched him aboard.

It was 9:54 A.M.

The man they had rescued was twenty-seven-year-old Jeff Wandich, owner of the vessel that had been reported overdue, *Sea Esta*.

According to a Coast Guard source, Wandich was asked what had happened. He replied that his boat had sunk. When he was asked where his boat sank, Wandich replied, "You mean you haven't found the other guys yet?"

He was talking about the three men who had been with him: David Madott, Omar Shearer, and Kent Munro, all twenty-five years of age, and each a resident of Mississauga, a suburb of Toronto.

A Coast Guard crewman shook his head—no. "We haven't seen anything."

Wandich told the crew that his boat had swamped at around 3 P.M. Friday while anchored over the *"California,"* a wreck that he and his friends had been diving. He said that his boat had finally sunk at around 7 P.M., and that he had become separated from the others while swimming toward the light tower. Wandich said that he had been on the tower since 11 P.M. Friday—thirty-five hours— and that he was very thirsty. He was sunburned, he had cuts on his hands and legs, and he appeared to be suffering from exposure.

When Wandich was offered the option of being flown to a hospital or remaining on station, Wandich said that he wanted the crew to continue its search. He told the crewmen that his three friends were all wearing wet suits and inflated BCDs—buoyancy compensator devices. "We should be able to find them," he said, and offered to help the crew get LORAN coordinates for the *"California"* wreck. (LORAN is an electronic navigational system that aids mariners in determining positions at sea.)

According to Wandich, a crewman told him they already had the coordinates for the wreck.

The helicopter crew, with Wandich aboard, found nothing. Nor did what, by now, was an even bigger Coast Guard search group.

Only Wandich would return to describe the events of November 4, and his story would catalyze both criticism and suspicion. In the weeks and months that followed, public gossip (often fueled by inaccurate media accounts) would accuse Wandich—as well as the three missing men—of crimes that ranged from fraud to smuggling to murder.

As Wandich would tell me much later, "People can say what they want about me, but the other three aren't here to defend themselves. They don't deserve that kind of talk. They were great guys—the best. We were . . . friends."

But his friends, David Madott, Kent Munro, and Omar Shearer, would never be seen or heard from again—even though they were all wearing wet suits and inflated buoyancy compensator vests. The rumors that still circulate around South Florida and Toronto echo the question asked of Wandich the morning he was spotted by a helicopter, standing naked on a light tower, fifty-two nautical miles out to sea: *What happened?*

David Madott and Omar Shearer had been best friends since grade school. Both were short, muscular extroverts. Both loved to play hockey—as did their mutual friends Jeff Wandich and Kent Munro—and they spent their free time together coaching youth hockey and soccer teams. Madott was employed by a Toronto auto parts manufacturer and, in just a few years, had quickly worked his way up the corporate ladder. Shearer was a chiropodist, or foot doctor. Some affectionately described the two as "carbon copies" not only because they were so much alike, but also because Madott was white and Shearer, whose family had moved from Jamaica when he was six, was black.

Kent Munro was a much bigger man—six two, 220 pounds—and he was a close friend of Shearer's from high school. Munro was quiet, soft-spoken, and the only one of the three who was married. All three men were viewed as "sports and fitness nuts" by their friends and families.

For Madott, Shearer, and Munro, flying to Florida to rendezvous with Wandich had been a spur-of-the-moment decision. It would be a chance to escape the bad weather and do some SCUBA diving. All three were certified divers, although Munro and Madott were new to the sport. They had arrived on Thursday, November 3, and would fly back to Toronto on Monday, November 7. Wandich's parents owned a residence on Marco Island, which lies 105 miles west across the Everglades from Miami. Marco is an affluent "planned" community: sodded lawns, CBS houses, beaches, golf courses, and high-rise hotels. Far to the north are Tampa and Orlando, and all the glitz that they imply, but immediately to the south lie the uninhabited Ten Thousand Islands and Everglades National Park—the largest roadless area in the United States. Wandich had offered them a place to stay on Marco and agreed to take them offshore in his twenty-five-foot boat, *Sea Esta*, to fish and dive.

As Wandich would say later, "They were just there for the weekend, and I wanted to show them a good time."

According to George Lampert, manager of Marco River Marina, Wandich and the three men left his docks around 8 A.M., fully fueled, but returned a short time later. Wandich told mechanic Lonnie Kienow that one of his twin 225-horsepower Johnson outboards behaved as if it were overheating. Kienow and Wandich took the boat for a test run, but both engines functioned normally. Kienow suggested that perhaps the engine's water intake had been temporarily fouled—not an uncommon occurrence with marine engines that have raw water pickups. Wandich, who had twelve years of occasional experience fishing and diving in the area, agreed. Even so, he purchased two Verna Therm thermostats to carry along as emergency replacements.

At a little after 9 A.M., with Kienow watching, the four men headed out into the Gulf of Mexico. Winds were blustery, seas less than two feet, water temperature seventy-seven degrees.

"The Wandiches took good care of that boat," Lampert says now. "It was in good shape when it left here."

That night after eight, Wandich's cousin, Ron Nayduk, telephoned the United States Coast Guard station at Fort Myers Beach and reported that the vessel *Sea Esta*, with crew of four, had been expected to return to Marco River Marina by 5 P.M., but was overdue. According to Nayduk, he told the Coast Guard that the men may have gone out to fish and dive on a wreck he identified as the *"California."* He says he also gave the Coast Guard LORAN numbers for the wreck.

The *Baja California* is a popular wreck among experienced divers. Wandich had dived it many times. On July 18, 1942, the 962-ton freighter was torpedoed by a German submarine and sank in 120 feet of water. It is located fifty-six nautical miles southwest of Marco Island in what is now a Naval Operations Training Area. Oddly, though, some popular nautical charts mistakenly identify the *Baja California* as two separate wrecks—*"Baja"* and *"California"*—with the *"Baja"* lying 8.97 nautical miles northeast of the *"California."*

This may or may not account for some of the confusion that followed.

At 9:52 P.M., the Coast Guard scrambled an H-60 helicopter out of its Clearwater air base. It arrived in the area before midnight. The LORAN numbers that Nayduk says he gave the Coast Guard are the exact coordinates for the actual *Baja California*. But whether the helicopter crew searched the *"Baja"* coordinates, the

"*California*" coordinates, or concentrated on some other area has become a subject of controversy. What is certain is that they found no sign of a boat, no debris, nor did they find the four missing men.

By the next day, Saturday, the search group had expanded to include the two H-60 helicopters, a C-130 fixed-wing aircraft, the Coast Guard's eighty-two-foot cutter *Point Swift*, and a forty-one-foot utility cruiser. The U.S. Coast Guard Auxiliary and other volunteers also provided boats and crew, but small vessels could not search offshore because the wind was now blowing twenty knots out of the east-southeast.

No traces of the boat or the men were found.

According to Fred Nayduk, the Coast Guard telephoned that afternoon or evening, and asked him to repeat the LORAN coordinates that Fred's son, Ron, had given the night before. "I had to call them back with the numbers," Nayduk said recently. "When I did, the guy from the Coast Guard said, 'Well, we've been looking pretty close to that area.' I told him that the '*California*' was only a few miles from a big light tower. I had been out there with Jeff several times. Ron had told them the same thing."

Nayduk was describing a 160-foot tower that lies 3.56 nautical miles east of the *Baja California*. But there are seven other such towers in the Naval Operations Training Area, and one looks like another. The towers are part of the military's Air Combat Maneuvering Instrumentation system, and are used by both the air force and the navy. The ACMI towers are equipped with strobe lights, electronic discs, and antennas, and they are maintained by the U.S. Department of Defense through private contractors. The towers are not shown on all charts.

The next morning, the Jayhawk rescued Wandich, and the search for the three missing men intensified.

The families of Madott, Shearer, and Munro flew in from Canada to augment the Coast Guard's efforts by organizing search vessels and aircraft from the private sector. They also offered a reward of $75,000 for the rescue or recovery of the three missing men.

They and the Coast Guard remained optimistic. "We have rescued people who have been in the water for four days in wet suits," one Coast Guard spokesperson was quoted as saying.

But by the fourth day, Tuesday, November 8, the Coast Guard had hunted more than 21,000 square miles of water on a carefully coordinated grid search. All that was found were Wandich's dive bag and video camera, both floating about twenty-one nautical miles southwest of the wreck site. Later, they would find two empty air tanks and a section of rope tied to an orange life jacket in roughly the same area.

On Thursday afternoon, November 10, marine salvage divers (not contracted by the family or the Coast Guard) towed in Wandich's boat, the *Sea Esta*. They had found it in 110 feet of water, lying upside down atop the *Baja California*, and had used air bags to refloat it and right it. That same day, Kent Munro's father, Peter—sleepless and distraught since the news of his son's disappearance—suffered a heart attack and had to be hospitalized in Fort Myers.

That night, the Coast Guard suspended what had been one of the most massive sea searches in the region's history. The Coast Guard had, in six days, covered 23,000 square miles of water with boats, planes, and helicopters but had found absolutely no trace of the three Canadians.

It was as if David Madott, Omar Shearer, and Kent Munro had ventured out onto a gray mountain, only to vanish into an abyss.

It seemed impossible. A common question was: how can three men in wet suits and brightly colored buoyancy compensator vests disappear without a trace? It just didn't make sense.

Something else that didn't make sense were certain data as reported by the news media. The Wandiches, the Munros, the

Shearers, and the Madotts are prominent families in their communities, and the Toronto press gave the event lengthy coverage, as did the Florida press. A consistent element in most of the stories was that it had taken Wandich four hours to swim from where his boat sank to the light tower—a distance that the Coast Guard had reported to the media was "six miles," though some media calculated it to be "nearly eight miles." (Six months later, this and other factual errors were still being parroted by the Toronto media.) However, these figures were accepted skeptically by people knowledgeable about boats and the Gulf of Mexico. To make such a swim in heavy seas, at night, was unlikely.

Some media also indirectly quoted Wandich as saying that "they"—he and his crew—had "forgotten" to use the *Sea Esta's* VHF radio to report that the boat was sinking.

To experienced boaters, this claim was not only unbelievable, it was outrageous.

In Toronto and Florida, sinister rumors began to circulate concerning the sinking of the *Sea Esta* and the disappearance of the men.

As a longtime member of the southwest Florida boating community, I heard most of those rumors. One rumor suggested that no one had actually seen the missing men leave port with Wandich. (It was never reported that mechanic Lonnie Kienow had watched them leave.) The rumor implied that Madott, Shearer, and Munro had either disappeared by choice, or that they had been killed. Either way, the sunken boat was a ruse. Another scenario relied upon the prevalent belief that the function of the ACMI towers was "classified" (it isn't), and that the military may have "eliminated" the men because they had seen something they shouldn't have seen. But the most common theory was that the men had really gone offshore to make a drug buy, but the deal had gone bad, and Wandich, the only survivor, was now afraid to tell the truth.

This rumor, I would learn later, was popular around Toronto. After all, Omar Shearer had been born in Jamaica, and his uncle, Hugh Shearer, had been prime minister of Jamaica from 1968 to 1972. Weren't Jamaica and the west coast of Florida both infamous drug depots? For many, no other evidence was required.

I was as suspicious as anyone else. As a waterman, the rumors I found most troubling were less tawdry but, in my mind, far more damning. I had heard that, when the boat was salvaged, its battery switch was in the "off" position. In most boats, this wouldn't affect the automatic bilge pump. But this boat, it was said, had been wired so that the whole system went dead when the switch was off. And why would a boat with twin engines have only one battery switch? I also heard that the scuppers (the vessel's raw water vent holes) had been plugged with plastic. Along with the general criticism and second-guessing that always accompanies boating accidents, these details in particular—if true—suggested foul play.

On Tuesday, November 22, a local Florida newspaper added grist to the rumor mill with a headline that read: "'Major Crime on High Seas' Suspected." The accompanying story reported that the FBI was now "investigating" the disappearance of Munro, Madott, and Shearer as a possible crime on the high seas. Despite the headline, the article did not quote any spokesperson from the FBI or the Coast Guard as saying that "a major crime on the high seas" was suspected. But this story—and similar stories that appeared in Toronto—confirmed what many were eager to believe. Jeff Wandich had been indicted and found guilty (of what, no one was quite sure) by the popular press. No other evidence was needed.

Wandich's distraught mother, Stella Wandich, was quoted as saying, "Am I supposed to feel guilty because my son is alive? I feel my son is being crucified."

But many doubted that her anger was justified because they believed that Wandich and, perhaps, Madott, Shearer, and Munro had been involved with some kind of illegal activity. To the credit of the families, they did not react publicly to the rumors, other than to say they had no reason to doubt Wandich's story.

As Bill Madott, David's father, told me recently, "Obviously we had a tremendous emotional interest in what had happened, but we also took pains to be open-minded about what could have happened. I had to take a very hard look at how well I knew my son— as did the others. Our inquiries all came back the same: the guys were not involved with drug running, and they had absolutely no reason to intentionally disappear. These were three genuinely nice guys who were happy in their lives."

Yet the rumors were now so widely believed that they had accumulated the patina of established fact. And pet theories continued to be promoted even as the families continued to search. By the end of November, they had invested half a million dollars in the effort. They had chartered planes, boats, and helicopters. They had consulted a French paramilitary intelligence expert, they hired a private investigator. They had even spoken with, and acted upon, the advice of psychics. "It just makes no sense that they all disappeared without a trace," Madott says. "One, maybe. Two, possibly. But not all three. We think it's possible that the guys were picked up by a vessel that, for political reasons, could not bring them back to the United States. Frankly, I don't care how or why Jeff's boat sank. I just want my son back."

More than anything else, it was the determination of the three families to find their children that fired my interest in the sinking of the *Sea Esta*. I am the father of two young sons, and to lose something so dear—without explanation or closure—was unthinkable. I would spend the next month researching the incident, interviewing key people, and would also travel to the site of the *Baja California* and dive the wreck. Ultimately, I formed personal conclusions about what happened on November 4.

But you should hear Jeff Wandich's story before you hear mine. . . .

Here is what Wandich says happened after he, Madott, Shearer, and Munro left Marco River Marina: "We stopped at a wreck *[Ben's Barge]* about three or four miles out in the Gulf to catch some bait because the guys wanted to fish and dive both. While we caught bait, we discussed where they wanted to go. Omar had fished the *'California,'* but he'd never dove it, so that's what they decided. We were listening to the weather channel on the radio, and I told them it wouldn't be real nice out there, but it should be okay."

According to the National Climatic Data Center, the forecast being issued that morning via VHF radio was: "From Cape Sable to Tarpon Springs, and fifty miles offshore, small craft should exercise caution. Winds will be out of the east fifteen to twenty knots, seas four to six feet, with bay and inland waters choppy."

Weather forecasts for the area aren't always reliable. Fishing guides often joke about them. But this forecast was accurate. The group headed offshore.

As Wandich tells the story now, several months later, his voice is soft, reflective. People who SCUBA dive deep water from small boats are prone to cockiness, but there is not a hint of that in Wandich. He is cordial, a little shy. There is a fabric of weariness in his voice; his silences seem to resonate.

"Once we got out there [to the *Baja California*] the seas were three, maybe three and a half foot. Sloppy, but not too bad. I anchored in the sand and drifted back over the wreck. It sometimes takes me three or four tries to get anchored just right, but that day, I did it on the first try."

(A common, though unsubstantiated, criticism of Wandich was the theory that he had anchored "into" the wreck—a common tactic of divers—and the short scope, or anchor line, had caused his boat to ship a wave and the line to break.)

"We fished for maybe an hour. You know how barracuda will crash a live bait right by the boat? The guys had fun with that. But it was getting a little rougher out and Kent started to feel sick, so we decided to gear up and get into the water because he would feel better then."

Wandich says that he paired up with Madott and that Shearer paired up with Munro because he and Shearer were the most experienced divers. The four men got in the water and started for the bottom. "I know that one of the laws of diving is that you never leave your boat unattended," Wandich says now. "I've seen other divers do it lots of times, and, the sad thing is, it was the first time I'd ever done it. We were fifty miles offshore, there weren't any other boats around, and I knew, because of the depth, our bottom time would be only about fifteen minutes. I had the dive flag up, and it never entered my mind that, in fifteen minutes, something could happen."

When the group got to a depth of about thirty feet, Wandich says Munro indicated that he was having trouble equalizing the pressure in his ears. "We sent Kent and Omar up to ten feet or so and had them come back down. But Kent's ears were still hurting him, I could tell. Omar indicated that he and Kent would return to the boat, and I signaled 'okay.' Dave and I watched them go to the surface, then we continued our dive."

Wandich says that he and Madott spent approximately thirteen minutes on the wreck, then started back up. When they were fifteen feet from the surface, they made a safety decompression stop of about three minutes. Then they surfaced. Wandich says he was shocked by what he saw.

"Only about three feet of the boat's bow was sticking out of the water. I couldn't believe it. Dave was in shock, too, and we started swimming toward the boat. We couldn't see Omar or Kent, and Dave yelled out Omar's name. Omar answered back to me, but we still couldn't see them because of the waves. The seas were running about four feet now.

"Dave swam straight to the boat while I swam toward Omar's voice. When I got closer, I could see him and Kent in the water, drifting away. They both had their BCDs inflated with the tanks still attached, but they weren't wearing them. They couldn't get back to the boat because they weren't wearing flippers, and the waves were pushing them farther and farther away." Wandich says he and Madott helped the two men jettison the tanks and get into their BCDs. They then swam back to the boat, jettisoned their own weight belts, and hung on to the unused portion of the anchor line that was attached to the bow. There, Wandich says, he checked his watch. It was 3 P.M.

"When things settled down," Wandich says, "our first question, of course, was what happened? Omar said he didn't know what happened. He said that he and Kent climbed up the dive ladder at the back of the boat and took off their BCDs and fins. Then he went to the front to take off the rest of his stuff. But he looked back and noticed water coming in over the transom, so he said he tried to start the motors. But the engines weren't going to start. The salvage divers told me later that, when they found the boat, it was still in gear. What must have happened was, I'd had Omar run the boat while I set the anchor, and he must have switched off the engines while they were still in forward.

"Omar said water was flooding over the transom and that then the boat started to tip sideways. He said it happened so fast, just like that, and that he and Kent jumped overboard. Dave asked Omar if he'd tried the [VHF] radio, but Omar got a little defensive, so we dropped the whole subject. I remember thinking to myself that, when we're back on land, we'll find out exactly what happened.

"The four of us just floated there, hanging on to the rope. The wind had picked up even more, and waves seem a lot bigger when you're in the water. But that was our plan: hang on to the rope, stay close to the boat, and wait for the Coast Guard to come and get us. Back on Marco, my girlfriend knew when we were due back, and she knew there were only a couple of places we could be."

For the next four hours, Wandich says, he and the three men floated on their backs alongside the boat, staying close to one another to keep warm. They tied an orange life jacket and a white bumper to the end of the rope. Madott also looped the rope into his flotation vest. The sun set at 5:38 P.M. and the new moon set an hour later. It was a black night, with stars hazed by scudding clouds.

"By the time it got dark, the wind was blowing pretty hard. I know I was scared, and I'm sure the guys were scared, too. But we kept the conversation light and tried to keep a cool head about everything. We talked about how this would be a story to tell our grandchildren. Someone said that we'd be best friends all our lives after this. We talked about girlfriends, things like that. The only one who didn't say much was Kent. He was a great guy, just quiet."

Then, at 7 P.M., according to Wandich, Omar Shearer yelled, "Where'd the boat go?" and the anchor line they were holding was ripped from their hands, pulling Madott, who was tied to the rope, under. Wandich says he was pulled under, too, and used his knife to cut the rope.

Several days later, the Coast Guard would find the cut line and life jacket more than twenty miles to the southwest.

"Omar must have been looking in that direction when the boat just disappeared," says Wandich. "It went completely down. We were in shock again, and I said, 'Let's go, we've gotta go.' Omar said, 'Where are we going?' That's when I told them that we would have to swim to the light tower."

Shearer was a more experienced diver than Kent Munro and David Madott, but he was not a strong swimmer. When he told the others that he didn't think he could swim that far, it was Madott, his childhood friend, who tried to reassure him, saying, "Omar, we don't have a choice. We'll make it. We'll all make it."

The four men set off swimming toward the powerful strobe on the ACMI tower 3.56 nautical miles (4.1 statute miles) to the east. They were swimming almost directly into the teeth of a twenty-knot wind and seas that had built to six feet. They were all wearing wet suits and inflated BCDs, but, according to Wandich, everything else had dumped out of the boat when it capsized and settled vertically, bow high—tackle boxes, fishing rods, weight belts . . . and Munro's and Shearer's fins.

"Dave and I still had our fins, but we all swam together," Wandich says. "We just plugged along, side by side, with me on one end and Dave on the other, Omar and Kent between us."

At this point in the story, Wandich's voice becomes even softer, seems less certain, and he has a difficult time controlling his emotions. "Time-wise now, what seemed like a long time probably was a short time. I'd say, roughly, about five minutes into the swim . . . we were just swimming, you know, and I . . . I remember being overcome with fear. I had tears in my eyes because I knew we were in a lot of trouble. There was another light way off to the south of the tower, like a boat, maybe. We could see it when we were on top of the waves, a long, long way away. So I turned toward that light just to sort of get myself under control, because I didn't want the guys to see that I had lost my composure. I heard Omar yell to me, 'Jeff, don't leave us,' and I said, 'I'm not,' and he said, 'You'll be safer here with us.'

"I guess he thought I was going toward the boat or something. But I wasn't. There was no place else to go but the tower. I wasn't far away from them, maybe ten feet . . . two waves away . . . and then I took a look to my left and . . . I didn't see them anymore. They were gone."

Wandich says he called out and started swimming toward where the men had been. "I'm almost positive I heard them yell back, but it was windy and loud, a lot of whitecaps. I treaded water for a little bit, but I never heard anything again. That's when I thought I was lost for sure."

After a short time, he says, he set off for the ACMI tower alone. Because he felt he wasn't making any headway against the waves, he soon jettisoned the face mask he still wore around his neck, and, finally, the BCD vest that kept him afloat. "I was desperate," he says. "The waves kept catching the BCD, pushing me back. I knew in my mind that I couldn't make it to the tower with the BCD on, and I didn't think there was much chance of one person floating alone being found. I don't know if taking off the vest was a dumb thing to do or a smart thing. But, in a way, I think it saved my life."

The ACMI's strobe flashes every four seconds. On a black night, it is a dazzling explosion of white light that, if watched even for only a few minutes, becomes hypnotic, and quickly perverts all sense of direction or depth of field. At 11 P.M., after four hours of swimming fixedly toward the strobe, Wandich climbed up the ladder onto the tower's lowest deck. "I lay down on the platform just to sort of reassure myself that I'd really made it. But, after a while, I got up and started calling for the guys. As the night went on, I kept thinking I heard them. The wind makes strange sounds out there. I kept getting up and calling back, calling their names."

Around midnight, Wandich saw what he correctly believed to be a Coast Guard helicopter off in the distance, with its searchlight fanning the water. He could also see the running lights of a boat far to the west near the *Baja California*. "My eyes just kept following the helicopter," he says. "It went east, then south a bit, and I just followed it around the tower. I watched it for a long time, and then it stayed out in the area where my boat went down, so I figured the boat lights were a Coast Guard cutter and they'd found the guys and were picking them up. I wanted to believe that. But then the boat seemed to head off to the southwest, so I figured they'd found my BCD and were looking for me now. Out there, your mind does strange things. I was trying to make sense of what the boat was doing because I wanted to believe it so much."

But the light he saw wasn't from a Coast Guard vessel. It was the *Great Getaway*, a ninety-foot charter boat out of Fort Myers Beach. Captain Ken Pearson had stopped to fish the *Baja California* while en route to the Dry Tortugas, fifty miles away. Pearson confirms that he, too, saw the Coast Guard helicopter.

"We first saw it when we were about ten miles north of the *Baja California*. It had its spotlight on, in a search pattern. They did a flyby of my boat, then continued searching. We anchored on the wreck at about one A.M. and fished for about an hour. The helicopter was in that area by then."

Wandich, who hadn't had anything to eat or drink since Friday morning, spent thirty-five hours on the tower, hearing noises, waving to boats, planes, and helicopters that never saw him until nine forty-five Sunday morning.

On December 7, I accompanied four professional divers and a private investigator to the wreck of the *Baja California*. They had been hired to bring up equipment and personal effects that had been lost when the *Sea Esta* sank. Ironically, the weather was very similar to the weather of November 4: wind out of the northeast at fifteen to twenty knots. Aboard our fifty-three-foot cruiser, the four-to-six-foot seas were unpleasant. In a twenty-five-foot boat, conditions would have been miserable.

By now, thirty-two days after the Canadians had disappeared, more people doubted Wandich's story than believed it—and, if he was telling the truth, they said, he had, at the very least, exercised horrible judgment. Around docks and marinas, the Coast Guard was getting its share of criticism, too. Watermen tend to be territorial. No outsider, they believe, can know the currents and quirks of their area like they know them—including the Coast Guard. Some critics said the Coast Guard was looking too far to the north. Others said the Coast Guard was looking too far to the south.

There were plenty of questions but few answers: had the Canadians really gone to the *Baja California* to fish and dive? Was the sinking accidental? Did Wandich exercise poor judgment? Did the Coast Guard mishandle the search? If not, why hadn't three men in inflated BCDs been found?

I hoped that the first question, at least, might be answered by retrieving the gear that the men had carried with them. We would spend a day, a night, and part of the next day on the wreck. In that time, our divers brought up twenty-four items that proved to be from the *Sea Esta*, including Wandich's black weight belt, Shearer's chartreuse weight belt, and Munro's orange weight belt. (Madott's weight belt had already been retrieved by the salvage divers who refloated the *Sea Esta*.) Wandich, unaware that his belt had been found, would later tell me how he had dropped it after returning to the swamped boat. We found it near the other belts—exactly where it should have been.

Our divers also brought up one SCUBA tank filled with air. Wandich said they had carried eight. The salvage divers, employed by Island Marine Towing, had retrieved two tanks that were nearly full (or they would not have sunk). And the Coast Guard had already recovered two air tanks drifting miles from the site. Air tanks that are empty, or nearly empty, float. It supported

Wandich's story that only he and Madott completed the dive, although three tanks were still unaccounted for.

Also recovered were an assortment of fishing rods, a big tackle box, and two smaller tackle boxes. They contained several hundred dollars' worth of tackle and lures, including some new lures still in cellophane. Would a man who planned to sink his own boat invest money in new lures? Two of the rods were light-tackle spinning rods, and one was still rigged with a number 3 hook—a hook size commonly used for catching bait. Wandich said that they had stopped on the way out to catch bait.

We also believed we had found *Sea Esta*'s anchor fouled in the *Baja California*, its line cut or snapped. It turned out, though, that the anchor belonged to Island Marine Towing. When the *Sea Esta* surfaced, Captain David Satterfield, who operates Marine Towing, says he had to cut his own anchor line to get *Sea Esta* drained and under way. The Wandich family has hard feelings toward Satterfield, who billed them nearly fifteen thousand dollars in salvage fees without first getting their okay to salvage the boat. In truth, Satterfield didn't need their approval. Since the Key West pirate days of the 1700s, marine salvage has been a controversial but legitimate enterprise in Florida. Success relies upon the misfortune of others, and salvage captains don't go into the business to make friends. Satterfield claims that, when his divers found *Sea Esta*, its anchor line had already been cut. Wandich insists that neither he nor his friends had any reason to cut the line, implying that Satterfield is more interested in the requirements of admiralty law than the truth. Wandich also correctly points out that his boat wouldn't have ended up on top of the *Baja California* if he had cut the anchor line. It would have drifted as it sank. "The line could have chafed in two after the boat sank," Satterfield suggests.

But the *Sea Esta*'s anchor was not to be found in the wreck, which buttresses Wandich's claim that he anchored off in the sand.

It is an eerie experience to dive through 110 feet of murky water, then come upon the colorful detritus of an event that led, most likely, to the loss of three lives. The old freighter was a fissure of rubble, the stillness of which implied a furious animation halted long ago. It might have been the remnants of a rock slide. It might have been a graveyard.

We also searched the bottom around the ACMI tower, but found nothing. In the end, our divers were convinced that the Canadians had come to the wreck to fish and dive—as was I. If they had wanted to buy drugs, why rendezvous at a wreck as popular as the *Baja California*? With LORAN or GPS electronics, any preagreed-upon spot in the Gulf could become a precise meeting place, without risk of interruption. Why go to the trouble of equipping themselves to fish *and* dive? One or the other would have provided sufficient camouflage. And, if the three Canadians had wanted to disappear, why would their friend, Wandich, intensify search efforts by saying they were wearing inflatable vests? The same would be true if he or someone else had killed them.

It made absolutely no sense. So why had the FBI "investigated" the case? Why had the print media run headlines alluding to a "major crime on the high seas"?

It wasn't until much later that I would find out that the FBI never mounted an investigation into the disappearances because the agency found no credible reason to investigate. As Brian Kensel, special agent, Tampa, told me recently, "In this case, there was an apparent unexplained loss of three lives. The Coast Guard asked us to take a routine look. They had found nothing to indicate that it was anything but a tragic accident. What we did was a preliminary inquiry but found no reason to open a full-fledged investigation. There was no evidence of any criminal wrongdoing."

A preliminary inquiry is not a matter of public record, so the FBI cannot confirm publicly, or privately, that Jeff Wandich was offered, and agreed to take, a polygraph test concerning the events of November 4.

"I wanted to take it," Wandich says now. "The guys' families never said anything to me, but I knew they had to have questions about what happened out there." Wandich says he spent more than four hours with a polygraph specialist. Special Agent Ray Vatkus was in charge of the inquiry. Upon completion, a source says that Wandich was told, "You've got nothing to worry about," adding, "the kid passed with flying colors. He was telling the truth."

Apparently, Stella Wandich's indignation was justified when she told the media, "I feel my son is being crucified." The unspoken indignation of the familes of the three missing men also becomes understandable.

Says Bill Madott, "People who believe the rumors about drugs or staging their disappearance can't possibly know anything about David or Omar or Kent."

So why did the *Sea Esta* sink? To understand, you need to know more about the *Sea Esta*.

The boat was built and rigged in 1989 by a small Miami manufacturer. The boat's back end, or transom, was cut very low to the water. Twin 225-horsepower Johnson engines, weighing 455 pounds each, were mounted on the transom. Abutting the transom were three deck hatches. Port and starboard hatches each contained a thirty-seven-pound marine battery. The center hatch was a baitwell plumbed to hold approximately twenty gallons of water, but would hold thirty gallons if the overflow tube was plugged—an additional 160 to 240 pounds.

Rigged the way she was, *Sea Esta*'s stern was weighed down by more than 1,200 pounds of water and hardware. Only eleven inches of freeboard plus a folding fiberglass spray curtain separated the cockpit from the open sea. Kent Munro and Omar Shearer, with dive gear, could have added 500-plus pounds—nearly a ton of weight.

Most offshore boats could handle this. But the *Sea Esta*'s scuppers were not covered by flanged flaps, which means water would flow in freely once pushed below sea level. Also, the port scupper gutter not only was half an inch off true, but it was also drilled half an inch lower on the transom than the starboard scupper. What this means is that there were several ways for water to come into the boat, but almost no way for it to get out.

There are several possible scenarios: a dead fish plugged the baitwell, yet the bait pump continued to pump and flooded the inner hull. If Munro and Shearer had climbed onto the stern at the same time, the additional weight could have swamped the hatches and shorted the batteries. Maybe one of them pushed down the fiberglass curtain to get their equipment aboard. Because it was over twenty-two feet in length, the *Sea Esta* was not required to have flotation, and it didn't.

The only thing surprising about the *Sea Esta*'s sinking on November 4 was that it hadn't already sunk.

And what about the battery switches? (There were two, not one.) Had the boat's electrical system, including the two bilge pumps, been switched off as rumored? David Satterfield is the only one who could have answered that question because he and his men removed the engines and the electronics twenty-four hours before anyone else inspected the boat. But Satterfield says he didn't check the switches. However, one man involved with the strip-down remembers a telling incident: "There were sparks when we removed the radio. And that was right after we got the boat in. It was getting juice." The wires could have fused and bypassed the switch, but, as several marine mechanics told me, that is extremely unlikely. Nor had the boat's plug been pulled, as rumored. Satterfield says, "The plug was definitely in. I didn't see anything to suggest that [Wandich] had intentionally sunk the boat." As George Lampert, of Marco River Marina, pointed out,

"Why would Jeff have bought the two engine thermostats if he didn't plan on coming back?"

No one familiar with the facts (and that includes the Coast Guard and the FBI) doubts that the sinking was accidental. Few also doubt that Wandich exercised questionable judgment. He had heard the weather report but went to the *Baja California* anyway. And he left his vessel unattended during the dive (although the trouble apparently started while Munro and Shearer were aboard). On Florida's west coast, because of the plethora of islands and shoal water, small boats are the conveyance of choice. It is not uncommon for owners of those boats to also use them offshore. I know a man who dived the *Baja California* out of a fourteen-foot boat, and I know several people with *Sea Esta*–size boats who regularly operate far from land. Dangerous? On the water, all calculations of risk are subjective. Satterfield—no friend of Wandich—summed it up accurately: "No matter how well you think you know the Gulf, you don't know it. And just when you think you do know it, it'll reach up and smack you in the face."

But, if Wandich made mistakes that day, he is not the only one. According to the Coast Guard's Search and Rescue Incident Phone Log, obtained through the Freedom of Information Act, Fort Myers Beach Coast Guard notified St. Petersburg headquarters of an overdue vessel, the *Sea Esta*, at 9:10 P.M. On the log, the position of the *"California"* as provided by Ron Nayduk is given. At the bottom corner of the log, someone has noted "[Station] believes that position is misplotted by [reporting source] as no wrecks at this position."

But there was a wreck at that position. It was the *Baja California*. The Coast Guard's recalculated position corresponds roughly with what has been mistakenly called the *"Baja"*—nearly nine nautical miles to the north.

This may seem like a critical error, but was it? If the rescue helicopter had flown directly to the site of the *Baja California*, it would have arrived more than four hours after the *Sea Esta* went down. Wandich had already arrived at the light tower by that time. Presumably, Munro, Shearer, and Madott were also far from the wreck. Even when the H-60 helicopter did arrive on-site (between midnight and 1 A.M.), the Coast Guard was looking for an overdue boat, not four men adrift on the night sea. It wasn't until Sunday morning that anyone knew that the boat had sunk. No one who reads the 140-page file on the incident can doubt that the Coast Guard invested a massive amount of time and resources into the search.

So why weren't the three Canadians found? One reason may be that their inflated buoyancy compensator vests weren't as "colorful" as most people assumed. Shearer's vest was blue, Madott's and Munro's were both black. The vests did not have reflective tape (as commercial flotation devices are required to have), and none was equipped with battery-operated strobe lights. Of the three, only Madott wore a brightly colored wet suit—it was fluorescent pink and blue with lime green panels. Shearer wore a sleeveless blue "farmer John" wet suit; Munro's wet suit was blue and black.

For me, the most telling—and most chilling—experiences while revisiting the *Baja California* occurred above the water, not below it. When we were within twenty miles of the site, I took a pair of binoculars and spent the next two hours scanning from the roof of the wheelhouse. As a father, it was a personal gesture of empathy to the fathers of the lost. Were the terrible circumstances reversed, I would have wanted them to do the same for me.

For an hour, I saw nothing; nothing but rolling gray waves and whitecaps on a shifting horizon. And then . . . for the briefest instant, I saw a flicker of green—lime green. It flashed, flashed again, then disappeared. David Madott's wet suit had had a lime green panel.

I banged on the roof of the wheelhouse. We brought the boat around and retraced the froth of our own wake. I had not moved my eyes from the place where I had seen the flicker of green, yet we could not seem to find it. Finally, we did: it was a lime green crab trap buoy, about the size of a man's head. We had passed within thirty yards of the thing, but if I had not been looking in exactly the right place, at precisely the right time, I would not have noticed it.

That afternoon, anchored on the wreck, our divers used a tractor tire inner tube to float a tool chest from the *Sea Esta*. I was in the water, waiting to swim the tire back to the boat. When the inner tube surfaced, men on our boat had to use hand signals to direct me toward it, for I never saw it. Then, as I swam farther and farther toward the drifting tire, I couldn't even see our fifty-three-foot boat unless I was on the crest of a wave. To be in the water, adrift on open ocean, is akin to tumbling slowly through the chasms of a gray mountain.

Why weren't the three men found? If you are ever in a boat in heavy seas, the cause will be all around you, but there will be no "reason," no dynamic that can be singled out and intellectualized. Open ocean is indifferent to fault or blame—concepts we on shore cling to for comfort. It is possible that some kind of outlaw commercial vessel rescued the men, but even the families of David Madott, Omar Shearer, and Kent Munro realize how unlikely that is.

"I know now that he is probably gone," says Omar's mother, Kathleen Shearer. "He was my youngest child. So affectionate, so full of life. But I still hold out hope."

As do the other families. The search continues and has been expanded to include Central America, Colombia, and Cuba, even as the families—and Jeff Wandich—struggle to come to terms with what occurred.

Wandich says now, "It's gotten a little better, but I'll never be able to get it out of my mind. It was awful; a terrible thing. I still dream about it. I dream about it every night."

When you have been lost on the gray mountain, nightmares don't always vanish with first light.

THE CURSE OF THE GIANT JAGUAR

Maybe through influence, but probably through curse, the Temple of the Giant Jaguar was the shaper of my personal policy on urban transportation. I can blame it, thank it, love it, hate it, but the policy remains as unyielding as ever. When I arrive in an unfamiliar city, any city, I lose all control of the itinerary. I store my gear, put two bottles of beer into a bucket of ice, then I go to the streets and run. Damn the cabs, the buses, the rickshaws and yak carts, I run. I run aimlessly, though not without purpose, and it doesn't matter if I am above the tree line or below the equator—which is why I'm pretty certain that I now travel under the effects of a terrible Mayan whammy.

It all started many years ago in the jungles of Guatemala, at the ancient city of Tikal. Located 190 miles north of Guatemala City, Tikal is a massive ruin of temples, shrines, and triumphal platforms. Before the birth of Christ, and up until about A.D. 900, this now silent place was a ceremonial center of the Maya, an astonishing people. Generations of craftsmen, mathematicians, priests, and their progeny lived, thrived, and died here. But now, when approached from the air, the only hints of long-gone human commerce are the bleached roof combs of pyramids that poke through the rain forest canopy.

I had been to Tikal twice in previous years, but on this particular trip, I came by Land Cruiser, not by plane. I was on my own, free to roam haphazardly among the remnants of 1,100 years of ceaseless construction. There were tour groups in the park—there always are—but I held my ground, for I had decided to select one small piece of Tikal and spend the whole day there. When I say "piece" I mean just that. There are six square miles of ruins, and it is numbing if one tries to see too much. The etched stonework soon blurs. Also, a Zen Buddhist friend had recently implied that I lacked spirituality—a ridiculous charge. Even so, I thought that by enduring several boring hours meditating over a single carving, I could prove to this curd eater that I was as spiritual as the next guy.

The area I chose was the Great Plaza, where the Temple of the Giant Jaguar faces the Temple of the Masks. Lying between is a lawn running east and west, on which are several stelae—carved stone markers—and it should have been easy to select an etching, then to sit in quiet communion with the brilliant Maya of long past.

But it wasn't easy. Tour groups kept queuing up, talking loudly. And the strolling beer salesmen wouldn't leave me alone. Stare as I would at the bizarre mosaics of animals with human heads, human bodies with jaguar faces, the weird feather-work on snakes, fish, and other strange creatures, I just couldn't concentrate. As reckoned by the Mayan calendar, I sat there for less than One Kin—in American time, the equivalent of about a six-pack. But daylight is not conducive to meditation; sitting quietly just invited interruption. And walking wasn't any better. I tried it. Which is when I made a fateful decision: I would return to the Temple of the Giant Jaguar that night and have the whole place to myself.

I should say right here that it is illegal to visit the pyramids after dark. Not only that, it is dangerous. As Carlos Ortiz, manager of the nearby Jungle Lodge, explained to me, an armed guard with a dog patrols the park grounds once the gates are locked. Not that I told Ortiz of my plans. This nice man wouldn't have allowed such lunacy. But I was determined to do it, and I did.

I left the Jungle Lodge at about 11 P.M., carrying only a Mini Maglite flashlight, though I did not use it to find my way. No. I didn't want to alert anyone. Above, there was no moon, but stars eddied in a black vacuum, which was light enough. It is about a mile from the lodge to the Great Plaza, and I took my time, walking slowly. I found the fence, climbed it, then felt my way along the earthen path that tunneled through the trees. There is a density to rain forest at night. The weight of it descends, and it is a little like walking under water. It was quiet, too; a crackling, whirring kind of quiet, like the sea bottom at two atmospheres, and I had to remind myself to breathe. But, soon, the tree canopy thinned. Stars reappeared. And then the Temple of the Giant Jaguar rose out of the gloom, a pyramid in silhouette against a scrim of deep space.

The Temple of the Giant Jaguar is nearly 150 feet high, and a ramp of stone steps leads to an open chamber at the top. I couldn't wait to get up those steps—not because I was eager to meditate, but because I was worried about the guard and his damn dog. They could have jumped me at any time back in the forest. But, once I got to the top of the pyramid, I'd be safe. What kind of dog would charge up several hundred steps just to bite someone? Certainly not one of those curly-tailed curs common in Central America. So I half walked, half crawled up the steps to the top of the pyramid and took a seat on the stone platform. I was above the tree canopy now. The rain forest of Peten rolled away in charcoal mist, and it was a little like sitting above the clouds. It should have been wonderful. From this distance, the jungle glittered with fireflies—millions of them, detonating randomly. There were so many fireflies that, visually, the effect became disturbing. My ears kept straining to hear the noise of those miniexplosions but, of course, there was only silence, a deep and complete silence, and I began to imagine that I had gone deaf.

I decided to change the mood by exploring inside the pyramid chamber. For the first time, I used my flashlight, shining it on the carved lintel above the middle doorway. After all, this is what I had come to do: ponder the strange etchings of the Maya. This wooden lintel, more than a thousand years old, was an extraordinary artifact. Carved into it were swirling feathers that seemed to form a human face. That figure was connected to an inlay of rectangular shapes that formed more human faces; a complex mosaic, each connected to the other. The longer I looked at it, the more faces appeared. Gazing at these long-dead people, just them and me up there alone in the dark, my true spiritual nature really kicked into gear. Also, it began to get a little spooky. There was a beautiful woman wearing a headdress. Her black eye held me, then dismissed me. And there was a nobleman with something coming out of his ear. A snake? Yes, a snake . . . and the snake seemed to be crawling toward the open mouth of . . . of a withered old hag who was . . . Gad! . . . who was copulating with a jaguar.

I backed away from the lintel, filled with a growing sense of foreboding. During the day, Tikal was as benign as a museum, but now, in darkness, it seemed an eerie reunion place of the ancient dominion. And I had the strong feeling that none of those lost souls wanted me there. I found the stairs and began to work my way down, slowly, slowly, because the old hag on the lintel had the fickle look of a practical joker. Tripping would have been fatal, but murder is small potatoes to anyone who would mate with an animal. Back on the ground, I began to walk calmly toward the

Jungle Lodge. I was no longer worried about the guard. I would have welcomed human company. And if the dog attacked . . . well, the old hag would know how to handle *him*, the poor bastard. Just thinking about her witchy face goaded me to walk faster . . . faster . . . until, soon, I was jogging . . . jogging because I had the terrible impression that all the grotesqueries of that place were rising up in my wake . . . jogging at a strong, steady pace, to hell with the darkness and the bad footing.

Once I kicked a log and fell, but I got right back up and began to jog again. And it was during that fast retreat to the lodge that I had a flash of realization: the instant I had started jogging, the forest ceased to be a weight above me; the ruins of Tikal were no longer a sinister presence behind me. The simple act of running had transformed my relationship with the surroundings. I felt safe in a sphere created by my own exertion, which was a wonderful feeling. I could still smell, hear, and see the forest, but I was doing it on my own terms. Sitting or walking seemed prissy in comparison. Spirituality? I'm still as spiritual as the next guy, which is to say that, if God or his long dead want to communicate with me, they can dial direct, day or night, just so long as they leave that jaguar humper out of the loop. Otherwise, I'll be out there running, emotionally bulletproof.

Which is precisely how my personal policy on urban transportation was shaped. An ancient city, an old city, a modern city—I now treat them all the same. As mentioned, the first thing I do upon arrival is store my gear, arrange for refreshments, then pull on shoes and shorts, and go for a run. An hour on the street cuts straight through the tourist brochure malarkey; it brings smells, sights, and sounds straight to the senses, no middleman. Tour buses? They're too confining, plus the guide always expects a tip. Same with cabs. A bicycle would be good, but where is one going to get a bicycle? Skates, ditto. And forget those low-impact walking tours—just too much risk of injuring an elderly person.

No, running is the best way to go. Prior to suffering the curse at the Temple of the Giant Jaguar, layovers in cities were sensory vacuums: hotel pools, clock watching, and dull museums. Now layovers pack a punch, little miniadventures with all kinds of potential. The trick is to go properly prepared, and with the right attitude. Remember, on a running tour, fitness is a peripheral benefit, not an objective. If you pass an interesting monument or shop, person, or pub, you are not only allowed to stop, you should stop. Also, never preplan your route. There is a karmic component to this kind of touring, so it is best to follow your instincts rather than a map. Because of this, the wise traveler carries equipment not commonly associated with 10K fun runs. I pack American greenbacks in my socks, no coins—too noisy, plus I still haven't figured out how to use foreign pay phones. I also carry my tourist card (police are prissy about identification), a compass, and a card bearing the name and address of my hotel (you'll see why). The little extra weight is worth it.

I have jogged through cities all over the world, and not so surprisingly, the most lasting impressions I have of those cities were collected while running. In my mind, Lima, Peru, is crumbling Castillian architecture and political graffiti on the walls of alleys where children, too hopeless to make eye contact, sleep on cardboard pallets. Managua, Nicaragua, is smog and traffic, rain-slick sidewalks and baseball fanatics eating *bocas* outside Mad Monk Stadium, waiting for the game to begin. Perth, Australia, is clean streets, safe parks, and black swans; Singapore is cleaner streets, even safer parks, and plenty of whack-happy rattan growing down by the river. Kota Kinabalu, Borneo, is bamboo forests on the outside of town, filthy rivers, and whole hillsides ablaze, slashed and burned.

Anchorage, Belize, Galway, Hong Kong, Kuala Lumpur, Medan, Quito, Havana, Sydney—these aren't just sterile cities anymore. They are side streets, the odors of suppers cooking, traffic, shopkeepers sweeping, a stranger's gaze from a balcony window, and other small intimacies. One of the great things about running is that there is no profit in bothering a runner. They are sweaty, walletless, and have too much momentum to mess with. On one of the few occasions that I was stopped, it was by a desperate man who didn't want money—just important information. The man taught me much about how Americans are perceived in the far corners of the earth, and it is just one example of how educational a running tour can be. This was in Nadi, on the west coast of Viti Levu, Fiji, where I had to lay over for a couple of days on my way to another destination. Nadi is not a pretty city. Because of the international airport there, it is a jumble of duty-free shops and cheap hotels that smell of pineapple and kava. Fiji lies between the equator and the tropic of Capricorn, so it is brutally hot; a terrible place to run at midday. But, as I said, the curse is unyielding, plus I was loony with jet lag, and jogging gave me something to do while waiting for the beer locker to open at my hotel. So I ran each day, and each time I ran, concerned strangers would stop their cars and ask polite questions before offering me rides. Why was I running in this heat? Was something chasing me?

Keep in mind that this kind of running is not sport. Road racing is for amateurs, and for certain situations where dogs are involved. I do not run fast, and I wouldn't even if I could—which I can't. This is explorationing in its most intimate form, with all the inherent risks implied, which is why I now carry the aforementioned equipment. To illustrate: last year, I arrived in the Vietnamese capitol of Hanoi, numbed by flight and too many stops in way too many cities. It was after dark when I got to my downtown hotel, and it was still dark when I awoke at 3 A.M. On the far side of the earth, 3 A.M. to 6 A.M. are peak jet lag hours. The brain is disoriented, but the body is ready to kick names and take butt. Two hours later I was still awake, but at least the window of my hotel room was beginning to pale, so I pulled on a sweatshirt, shorts, and shoes, and went outside for my get-acquainted run. January in Hanoi is cold, and this happened to be January. It was misting rain, too. Through the gloom, streetlights showed yellow wedges of road, so I jogged from wedge to wedge. I didn't mind getting wet. Anything is better than being alone in a hotel room, wrestling with jet lag.

Gradually, over twenty minutes, the fog became radiant. Somewhere, the sun was up. I began to recognize shapes. There were trees, there were old men pushing carts, there were people by a lake doing tai chi, a traditional morning exercise, and there was a pagoda on the lake with a big red star affixed to it: thus I knew I was in some kind of public park. I ran through the park, crisscrossed some narrow streets, then decided to head back to my hotel. To do that, I believed, I had to first return to the park. But I couldn't find the park. I tried to retrace my route, but all the streets looked the same. By now, the fog had lifted, but it was still raining. I had been running for forty-five minutes, so I slowed to a walk and began to take seriously the job of finding that damn park.

No luck. The thing had disappeared; evaporated with the fog. I tried to ask for directions, but no one I met spoke English, and my pantomime of trees and tai chi only produced nervous laughter. I spent another half hour searching, then decided enough was enough, it was time to get a cab. I didn't have any money, but the driver would certainly be willing to wait while I went to my room for cash. And that's when I had a terrible realization: I didn't know the name of my hotel. Worse, I wouldn't recognize the place if I saw it because I had arrived at night and left before first light.

It is an awful thing to be alone, lost, and penniless in a big city, especially when one is soaked to the bone, wearing nothing but running clothes. And it is humiliating to wander from hotel to hotel, asking desk clerks, "Do you recognize me? Am I staying here?" Luckily for me, I met an Australian who seemed happy to spend two hours chauffeuring me from door to door, but one should never plan on such good fortune. That's why I now always run with a card bearing the name of my hotel, personal identification, and plenty of money for refreshments. This equipage is imperative, for the curse of the Temple of the Giant Jaguar is without sympathy, and maps don't come with this terrible Mayan whammy.

SHINE FORBES

Considering the tragic possibilities, considering the humiliation I endured, Lorian Hemingway might now be reluctant to admit that it was *she* who finagled me into fighting her grandfather Ernest's favorite sparring partner, Kermit "Shine" Forbes, on the docks of Key West where every sun-giddy Buckeye and dope fiend and pathetic wandering Parrot Head could watch and, potentially, testify against me if the worst happened and the coroner started sniffing around.

"The man is eighty years old," I reminded her.

"Exactly," she said. "Shine's a professional fighter with a lifetime of experience. He was more than a match for Ernest."

"Yeah, but we're talking about a very old guy."

Lorian said, "No, we're talking about Shine Forbes. Have you ever met the man?"

I didn't have to. I live in Florida where invalid octogenarians are only slightly less common than dead German tourists.

I said, "What happens if I miss and actually hit the guy? You know—out there clowning around, he moves the wrong way, and I coldcock him? Gad! My picture would be tacked like a wanted poster on every nursing home wall. Old ladies would thump me with their canes. I'd have to drive to *Georgia* just to buy groceries."

"Coldcock Shine?" Lorian has the ability to convey the unequivocal through laughter. Perhaps that is why she is a novelist—a gifted one—rather than a torch singer. "If someone moves the wrong way, it'll be you, not Shine Forbes. He's still all muscle, and he's still got the moves. But if you're afraid he'll hurt you—"

"Hah! Manipulation won't work, Lorian. At least one of us knows how smart I am, and I'm pretty sure it's me."

Lorian said, "Huh . . . ?," temporarily puzzled, before she continued: "All I'm saying is that I told Shine about you. That you used to box a little, but that you're big and clumsy and not too proficient. So he said he'd try to take it easy."

"Sure he did."

"And that he'd already heard how slow you are—"

"Hey—the old bastard said *that*?"

"Yes, and he'd carry you if it was necessary. *To carry* is a boxing term—"

"I *know* it's a boxing term. Look"—I was starting to get angry—"you don't know diddly about old people. It's because you live in the Pacific Northwest where every Big Band Era survivor either drowned or was eaten long ago. Personally, I've had just about a bellyful of their act. They win a couple of wars, invent space flight, then act like they rule the world. You ever seen how they drive? Run a simple red light, forget to use your turn signal, they'll honk and flip you the bird! Seriously."

Lorian said, "Three rounds, ten-ounce gloves. You and Shine on the docks just down from Sloppy Joe's Bar. Are you game?"

I asked a couple of questions first—Did the man use a walker? Could he be lying about his age?—before I told Lorian, "Rap on his hearing aid a few times, then tell Mr. Forbes I'm at his service."

Lorian seemed pleased. "Shine in an exhibition fight—Ernest might've gotten a kick out of that. It'll be a nice addition to the Hemingway Days Festival."

Hemingway Days Festival, indeed . . .

Every summer, second weekend in July, Key West hosts ten nonstop days of Hemingwayesque events, a few of them literary, but the rest of them are interesting and often fun. Hemingway Days is not to be confused with Key West's other create-cash-flow events such as the Gator Club Dolphin Derby, the Key West Womenfest, the Goombay Festival, and, especially, Fantasy Fest—a truly weird and twisted masquerade orgy, after which the fire department has to hose the streets just so it's safe for the sanitation boys to begin their dangerous cleanup work.

No, *this* festival has an honest theme. In the late 1920s and 1930s, Hemingway lived and worked on the island and has, by proxy of name and his descendants, been paying the chamber of commerce exorbitant rent ever since. The festival features the Hemingway Flats Tournament, Hemingway Fish Fry, Cayo Hueso Arm Wrestling Contest, Leicester Hemingway Storytelling Contest, Hemingway Trivia Contest, the Papa Hemingway Look-Alike Contest, Hemingway Golf Tournament, Hemingway Regatta, plus a music festival called the Moveable Musical Feast. Add to this a national short-story contest, a national first-novel contest, lots of writing workshops, tours, and readings, plus the annual Conch Republic Prize for Literature (Russell Banks won this year; Peter Matthiessen in 1995), and there is reason enough to visit an island that seems to offer—or possess—less and less *reason* as the years pass because of its willy-nilly descent into tourist whoredom.

Yes, to enjoy Key West these days, one must emulate the island's happy inner sanctum of society: ignore the chemically challenged, avoid Margaritaville and its Buffett pretenders, spend a lot of time on the water, and shun, at all cost, the geek magnet and drunk hatchery called Duval Street.

But I didn't come to enjoy Key West. I came to fight. And, because my first order of business was to meet my opponent (Know thy enemy), I went straight down Duval, turned west past an old two-story restaurant called Blue Heaven, and pretty soon was knocking on the door of a conch bungalow, the outside of which looked to be part museum, part art gallery.

I expected to be greeted by a doddering old casualty of the ring. Instead I was welcomed by . . . well, I'll admit it—by an extraordinary being; a man of wit and humor who was active as hell and as unpretentious as he was gracious. Yeah, and he still had the look, tendons, and veins that moved independently beneath skin, a fast-twitch muscularity . . . not good news.

Shine Forbes said to me, "Hey, man, get yourself in here! Want an Old Milwaukee?"

"Sure."

"I'm ready to go a couple rounds now!" Looking forward to it, he began to dance around snapping jabs at me. Good jabs, too.

Amazing. This guy was *eighty*?

Shine said to me, "Yeah, man, Mr. Ernest and me, we used to go 'round and 'round."

Now we were at Sloppy Joe's Bar and he was telling me about it. We were crammed in near the judge's table for the Hemingway Look-Alike Contest—lots of gray-bearded Papas peering down from the stage—but everyone allowed Shine, who'd *lived* it, his own respectful space.

It was a time-warp situation—Sloppy Joe's, all these guys in safari clothes. Very strange. Looking at Shine, I had to keep reminding myself that he was real: this man once boxed with *Ernest Hemingway. . . .*

Wrong—not once but many times. Put the gloves on beside the saltwater pool behind Ernest's house on Whitehead Street and laid some leather on the great man's beezer, the two of them buddies and probably closer than F. Scott Fitzgerald ever thought of being once they, Shine and EH, were under the spell of that lunatic sport.

Shine said, "Now Ernest, he didn't go 'round looking for trouble like some says. No-o-o-o, he weren't like me."

Shine, a troublemaker?

He shook his head. "This one time, yeah—the way I met him. I was very rude. You 'member the place by my house, the Blue Heaven?"

Sure. Old blue two-story conch building, probably built by shipwrights and now a restaurant.

"What the Blue Heaven used to be was a pool hall. Not with street ladies like some says—no the whores, they was over on Petrone Street, the House of Ornations. That what *that* place called. The Blue Heaven was a sporting house where we'd put on boxing shows. On a Friday, every two weeks us boys, we'd fight and make a little change.

"This one night, this big ol' man come down to referee. I didn't know who he was. Well . . . I was in Black Pie's corner. Black Pie, he was fighting Joe Mills, and Joe, he was beating Black Pie so bad I threw in the towel. What's this referee do? He picks the towel up and throws it back, hits me right in the face." Shine, wearing a Sloppy Joe's muscle shirt, his left eye droopy from so many fights, had to smile, remembering it. "So I take the towel and throw it in *again*. Same thing. Referee throws it back, hits me right in the damn face. Made me mad, man! I had a little of this in me"—Shine indicated the bottle of Budweiser in his hand—"which is no excuse for what I did."

What Shine did was vault over the ropes and take a swing at the referee.

"That man, he so big, he could'a hurt me. But no, he just blocked me," Shine said, "kind'a held me off till the other boys could pull me away. Man, I was *mad*. Somebody said, 'Hey, you want us to take this man to jail?' But the referee said, 'Uh-uh, anybody got the nerve to take a swing at me, I don't want him in no jail.' Kind'a calming everybody down, understand? That's when somebody, I don't know who—maybe Iron Baby; could'a been him—he take me aside and he says, 'Hey, man. You know who that referee is? *That* Ernest Hemingway.' "

Shine and a friend of his, Echo Sweden, walked over to Hemingway's house later that night to apologize.

"That when Mr. Ernest, he invited me and a couple others to come over, do a little sparring with him. Ernest, he was a real gentleman about it."

Shine became a regular at Hemingway's house. "We'd take turns with him, three rounds each. He weren't no real boxer, just did it for sport, see? But he so big, you could hit the man all day and not hurt him. And he'd pull his punches on us. We wore these big sixteen-ounce gloves and we'd kind'a *bounce* off him. Only this one time, I got under him and was working inside and he let one go and knocked me down. Didn't hurt me, understand, but what I'm saying is, the man could *hit*, he wanted to."

This was back in the mid- and late 1930s when Shine was in his teens and early twenties. "Times was tough for us back then," Shine told me. "One Christmas Eve, we didn't even have change for a quarter, so Ernest let us put on a boxing show at his house. It was Black Bob, Black Pie, Iron Baby, and me, with a bunch of Ernest's rich friends there to watch. Gene Tunney, he was there, and Lawyer Brooks, too—he 'bout the greatest lawyer Key West ever put out. After we done boxing, Ernest, he passed the hat, and it had over two hundred dollars in it. That was some *good* Christmas."

Shine said, "Then one day, he just left. Ernest, I'm talking about. They said he moved to Cuba or something, I don't know. But we sure missed him. He was a good man. He was sure good to us."

The Hemingway Look-Alike Contest wasn't done—there was a "Hemingway" onstage right now, carrying a stringer of fresh dorado to impress the judges—but Shine had had enough.

Leaving (he wanted to drive me around in his old car, show me some Key West shortcuts), he said, "I'm not the kind to stand around and drink, drink, drink, man. I know when I got enough." Shine said, "I know when I got enough of anything."

The day of the fight, here's what I was worried about: I didn't mind contributing to the Hemingway Days burlesque. Some wore beards and carried dorado on a stringer. Others put on boxing gloves. What I wouldn't do (nor would the Hemingway family, particularly Lorian, allow it) was play a role in some sideshow event in which Shine was diminished. The man had too much class. Unlike most things in Key West, he was . . . *real*.

That afternoon, I took him aside and talked about it. No . . . actually, we talked about it as I followed him around Duval Street, going from boutique to boutique, looking for a pair of shorts he wanted to buy for the fight.

At one of the shops, he said to the saleswoman, "You speak nothin' but that French, how you expect to sell anything to us Americans?" At another, where a salesman with earrings and red fingernails danced his way down the aisle, Shine whispered, "Lord'a mercy, back outta here, *back* outta here. You think I'm gonna let that boy measure *me* for somethin'?"

What I told him was that our "fight" was just an exhibition. "We're pretending to fight," I said. "People want to see you."

Shine was considering a pair of shorts—metallic silver material with blue and red stars. "You believe this?" he said. "Forty-five bucks for these? I can get me a nice *suit* for that."

I pressed the point. "What I'm saying is the whole thing's fake. I want you to know what you're getting into. Nobody expects us to really box. It's more like . . . theater."

Shine gave it a few beats, looking at me as if slightly pained. Finally, he said, "Gawdamn, Randy, you don't think I *know* that? Like a show, right?" Now he was laughing at me. "Man, I was putting on boxin' shows maybe before your daddy was born, so you don't need to say no more about *that*. Sure . . . we put the gloves on, dance around a bit, pull our punches like with Ernest. Yeah, man . . . make the people happy. I know *exactly* what that is."

Later that afternoon, on the Ocean Key House docks, I boxed three one-minute rounds with Kermit "Shine" Forbes, Ernest Hemingway's old sparring partner. Our audience—mostly fans of great literature—grew as the fight continued and came to include a typically Key West cast of sun-giddy Buckeyes, pathetic Parrot Heads, and maybe a few still living, breathing German tourists, too.

Jeffrey Lindsey, author of *Tropical Depression* and *Color Change*, was the referee. The man had flair: "Representing *Outside* magazine, desperately overweight at two hundred and twenty pounds . . ."

Lorian was my cornerman. ("You've got a cold, so I'd prefer not to wipe the sweat off you.") And an editor at *Oxford American* magazine ably worked Shine's corner. ("Go for Randy's belly. He had barbecue for lunch.")

The first round, when I threw my first punch, Shine picked it clean and said, "Hey, hey, *hey* . . . pretty stiff jab you got there, boy!"

I said, "Boy . . . ? I hope you said *Roy*."

Shine liked that; started laughing. "Then come on, Roy. Let's mix it up some."

We did, too. Lots of fake lefts and rights, then bear hugs with body shots. But every now and then, Shine would jab and follow with a right that touched my jaw or cheek, just to let me know who I was dealing with . . . reminding me who he was; used his gloves like a secret communiqué, telling no one but me—just me—that, yeah, man, I can *still* do it. . . .

He could, too.

The judges (they didn't have to wear tweed for us to see they were all literary types) gave the first and second rounds to Shine, ten to eight. Then, in the third, I rallied with a flurry of body shots, only to be knocked to the deck by Shine's big right hand. When Lindsey, the referee, got me to my feet, he studied my eyes and asked, "You okay? Where are you?"

I surveyed the area—turquoise water, purple sunset, freaks juggling torches over at Mallory Docks. "Dubuque?" I guessed.

Lindsey waved his arms—fight over. "The winner by a knockout, twenty seconds into the third round—Mr. Shine Forbes!"

And Shine stood there grinning, hands over his head, enjoying the way the people were enjoying it, part of a long, long show in which he'd always known precisely who he was . . . then he glanced at me and winked—this old guy who looked like he ruled the world . . . and deserved to.

CUBA

Land, sea, or air, ninety miles is ninety miles, except when describing the water space between Havana and Key West, a distance protracted by a generation of despair. Lately, men and women have taken to launching inner tubes beyond the landfall beacon off Morro Castle and paddling north. Crossing the Florida Straits in a Hatteras is one thing, but attempting it in a rubber doughnut, one's legs fluttering through the bright skin of the abyss, is a whole different proposition. In Cuba, desperation frames crazy optimism, or there is no optimism at all.

From my room on seventh floor of the Hotel Nacional, I could look down on the Malecón, the avenue that traces Havana's waterfront. Beyond the flow of bicycles, a few old cars, and aimless pedestrians, there was the sea, inflated with gray light. A streak of indigo marks the Gulf Stream's edge—it sweeps in close to Havana Harbor—and there were men in inner tubes fishing the rim of it, as if fishing the bank of a river. There was no fuel for boats, so they floated out in inner tubes. Except in the tourist hotels, there was almost no food, so they caught fish, or tried to. There weren't many fish. A few weeks of living like that, and I myself—not the bravest of men—would consider worming into an inner tube and paddling north toward Duval Street.

Sometimes, distance has resonance. Maps are deceptive.

Even for a tourist, it's tough to get out of Havana. Oh, it's easy enough to stop in the hotel lobby and book a sight-seeing shuttle to the beaches of Santa Maria, or into the tobacco country of Pinar del Río, or a flight to the dive resort on the Isle of Pines, or take a cab to Cuba's new vacation showplace, Veradero Beach. All it takes is money. American money. Lots and lots of American money, cash only. But what I wanted to do was get a rental car and drive south to a remote place called the Zapata Peninsula, a great landmass shaped like a shoe and shown as swamp on the map. I had heard rumors that portions of this swamp were, biologically, a mirror of the Florida Everglades, a sawgrass region commonly described as "unique" by observers—myself included. For more than twenty years, I have lived in or near the Florida Everglades system. I have hiked it, boated it, camped it, slogged it, studied it, and written about it, convinced—perhaps naively so—that it was the only sawgrass system of its kind in the world. Was there a similar Everglades in Cuba? That is what I wanted to find out.

But here's what happened on my first attempt to drive there: I landed at José Martí Airport in the late afternoon and stopped at the government's reception booth, where I bought two pretty good maps. The workers there wanted to know if I needed a hotel in downtown Havana, twenty minutes away. Or perhaps they could arrange a tour for me?

No, I told them, I only needed a car. There were still a couple of hours of daylight left. I figured I could make it most of the way to the Zapata Peninsula by sunset. Besides, I had been to Havana in 1977 on a SCUBA trip to the Isle of Pines, then again in 1980 during the Mariel boatlift. There were things I liked about Havana, but a city is a city, whereas a swamp is a good place to spend time.

The workers puzzled over my open maps. They seemed disoriented—or perhaps it was me. I am often disoriented when traveling, so tend to trust the advice of others. I pointed to the village of Playa Larga, 145 miles southeast of Havana, on the Bay of Pigs at the eastern fringe of the Zapata Peninsula.

Impossible, said one of the workers. There was no place to stay at Playa Larga.

I pointed to Playa Calmito on the western fringe.

No place to stay there, either. Wouldn't it be better if they booked a tour for me to another area? That way I could stay at a nice hotel in Havana and ride the tour buses each day.

The harder they pushed for Havana, the more determined I was to avoid it. I didn't need a hotel to sleep, and I could provision myself from the small villages through which I passed—that was possible, wasn't it?

The workers still seemed disoriented, peering at the map from odd angles. Perhaps, they said. Perhaps . . .

The Cuban rental car agency was in a building the size of a shed. It was a popular place with the locals because it had a window air conditioner. I attempted to negotiate for a car amid the noise and cigarette smoke. The man in charge was pleasant, but there was no negotiating: fifty-three dollars a day for a small Nissan, sixty free miles, but fifty cents a mile after that. Expensive, but there were no alternatives. The price, fixed by the government, would be the same no matter where I tried. The idlers inside watched me sign the contract. Among them was a prostitute named Evelina, a girl of about nineteen, who shadowed every move I made. She wore a red blouse and green spandex shorts. Her face was very pretty, everything else about her was old. When I ducked under the hood to check the car's oil, Evelina ducked with me. When I checked the spare tire in the trunk, she checked, too. I began to worry that Evelina came with the car, hired some- where in the contract's small print. She kept asking for a ride. When I said I was not going to Havana, she took the map and studied the marks I had made on it. Her expression was a mixture of fascination and confusion—a reaction parroted by every Cuban I asked for directions. No one seemed to know where they were. The map showed a world that was too big. The rental car building, with its window air conditioner, did not exist on the map, and Evelina was lost without it.

I left Evelina standing on the curb, her face floating in the rearview mirror. I drove out into the late-afternoon bicycle traf- fic—Cuba is now a bicycle society and, in this way, resembles Asia. It is a wonderful feeling to be under way in an unfamiliar country, alone and on the move, and I would have felt great, but for one thing: my car had no gas. I had paid five dollars for five liters (slightly more than a gallon) at the agency, but had not seen it put in, and the gas gauge showed below empty.

I stopped at the first service station. It was closed. So was the second. There was an attendant at the third, but they had no gas. Same at the fourth station. By now, I was miles from the rental agency and faced the possibility—the probability, really—that I would have to push my fifty-three-dollar-a-day car to Zapata.

I headed back to the rental car agency, coasting when I could. I got my money back. Evelina seemed happy to see me, but not very surprised. I left her and the rental car, taking a cab . . . into Havana.

It is illegal for an American to spend money in Cuba unless the American is a journalist, or has relatives living there and gets spe- cial dispensation from the Department of the Treasury. I had flown in through one of the common illegal routes, booking my Cubana

Airlines flight in Nassau, but I was still a journalist. And I was certainly spending money. A night in a simple room at the Hotel Nacional, the old Meyer Lansky brothel, cost $190, so it was while looking for a cheaper place that I met Monroe. Monroe was a Canadian, a veteran, and a lawyer—an outlandish trinity that complemented his outlandish personality. Though a small man, he cut a swath in his white sports coat, hair slicked back, his Ricky Ricardo mustache trimmed neat. When he walked, he sometimes limped. ("An old war wound.") He was always firing off faxes. ("The damn publisher keeps asking for my book!") He smoked Cohiba cigars but preferred the Trinidads he said were given to him by Fidel Castro. For the last year, he had spent every other month in Havana, making important business connections in preparation for the switch to free enterprise that he said must inevitably come to Cuba.

"It can't go on like this," he told me. "When it changes, I'll be ready and waiting. The money will flood in. I'll buy a mansion east of town, hire servants and winter here."

When Monroe wasn't hurrying off to meetings with high government officials, he could usually be found in the patio bar of the Havana Libre Hotel entertaining Cuban foreign ministers or ogling the prostitutes that swarmed the place. Monroe was at ease with the dignitaries, but the prostitutes troubled him. Late one night he said, "I haven't been with one of those girls. You won't catch me paying twenty bucks and sneaking out to the swimming pool! I have a fiancée, for God's sake!" It was less an observation than a declaration. He seemed to be trying to convince himself.

I don't know how much of what Monroe told me was true, but I liked him. He was smart, savvy, and I recognized his affectations and talking jags for what they were: the guy was homesick, hotel weary, and half crazy from living as an expatriate in Havana—though it was certainly better to live in Havana as an expatriate than as a subject. For us there was at least food to buy. Monroe knew the few bars and restaurants still open—all tourist places—and everyone at the bars and restaurants knew him. At La Floridita, a bronze bust of Hemingway watched us drink daiquiris. At La Bodequita del Medio, we ate black beans and chewed the fresh mint in our *mojitos*. Outside, the children begged for coins, the men begged us to buy black market cigars, and the women winked and pressed their breasts into our arms.

Monroe would say, "This city is part museum, part whore, and part bombing range. Don't the collapsed buildings remind you of Dresden? But all I have to do is stick it out. Do my work and keep to my routine. A month isn't very long. Havana is going to boom again, and when it does, I'll be rich."

Monroe, like everyone else in Havana, was waiting for something.

One night I met Carlos Calvo, a right fielder on the national baseball team, and he invited me to his practice the next day. I took a cab to the sports center, the Ciudad Deportiva, where Carlos met me, explaining that his team hadn't shown up, that practice had apparently been canceled. He shrugged, adding, "This is Cuba. Who can say why?"

Instead, the two of us sat and watched tryouts for the national fifteen- and sixteen-year-old team: thirty skinny kids dressed in rags, no spikes, hitting without helmets, sharing their cheap Batos ball gloves, but playing like I have never seen kids play before. It wasn't so much the skill—though they certainly had skill—it was the passion with which they played that was stunning; a kind of controlled frenzy that made their sullen coaches appear almost meek in comparison.

Carlos was unimpressed. Perhaps that kind of fervor was common in Cuban ballparks. Or perhaps one of these kids would someday try to take his job, so Carlos chose not to acknowledge them. He seemed more concerned with the condition of the field. The diamond was pitted with holes, weeds were knee-high in the outfield. "They used to mow it," he told me more than once. "I don't know why they don't mow it now."

That night, I found Monroe at his table in the patio bar. He was drinking daiquiris, which was unusual. Monroe drank very little, and never at night. It wasn't part of his routine. He told me about his business dealings that day, ordering two more rounds as he did, and as I arose to leave, he said, "I never do this, but one more daiquiri and I'll be drunk. Over the line." Naturally, I told the waiter to bring Monroe one more daiquiri before I headed off to bed.

At first light, I was awakened by pounding at my door. It was a haggard, wild-eyed Monroe. "Where were you when I needed you?" he rasped. "I was almost killed last night. Electrocuted!"

I tried to calm him. He sat and explained that he had gotten very drunk and stumbled off past the hotel pool in search of a place to urinate, but had brushed into some bare electrical wires. He showed me two black burns on his forearm that looked more like a vampire bite. The shock had knocked him unconscious, he said, but, luckily, one of the staff found him and managed to revive him.

"I banged and banged on your door," he said. "I was having trouble breathing. I needed help, and the hospitals here are worthless!"

I hadn't heard any banging. And I was suspicious of Monroe's strange story. Why had he wandered outside to whiz when the hotel's rest rooms were inside? I listened to him rage on about the management's liability. ("I'd sue them into bankruptcy back in the States!") His anger was real, but his account of what had happened was filled with holes. I suggested he show me the bare electrical wires. He was reluctant, but I pressed the issue. We took the elevator to the pool, and I followed Monroe to a wooden gate that was tied shut.

"Right through there," he said. "But the gate wasn't tied last night."

The gate led to a cramped space behind a row of cabanas. The space was not more than a yard wide. There were water pipes there and a jumble of spliced electrical wires. But for Monroe to have touched the wires with his forearm, he would have had to have been lying down . . . or kneeling.

I looked from the wires to Monroe. Monroe looked at the ground. "I know," he said, finally, "I know." He sounded exhausted, deflated. "I shouldn't have lied to you, and I shouldn't have done it. But she was so beautiful. You've seen those girls in the bar. My God! And how many months have I been fighting it?"

It was an astonishing event to re-create: coition interrupted by a charge of electricity and a shower of sparks. I found it hilarious—hilarious in a way that squeezes the heart—but Monroe would not be consoled. "I swore I'd never do anything like that," he moaned. "I'm here strictly on business. I have a routine! But this damn city does something to you. Believe me, Randy, it's this damn city!"

I had not given up on looking for the Cuban Everglades. I spent time talking to people in the bookstores near the University of Havana. It was extraordinary how little they knew of regions outside the city. I might have been asking them about the dark side of the moon. I did learn that there was a small resort on the Bay of Pigs at Playa Larga—but it was closed. "Broken," I was told, for their English was often better than my poor Spanish. The hotel at Mariel Harbor was "broken," too, as were several others. I got the impression that the Cuban government was funneling its shrinking food supply into only the most expensive, popular resorts and closing the rest.

Even so, when I finally did find a place to buy gas, I rented a Daihatsu, spent forty-seven dollars to fill its small tank, and headed off southeast on A-1, the country's main highway. I had slept in cars before, and I could provision along the way. Anything to get out of Havana. Not that it wasn't an interesting city, but a kind of melancholy pervaded the place; a melancholy illustrated by the circumstances of its people. Everywhere I went, there were men and women waiting in lines. There were lines to get water, lines to have cheap cigarette lighters repaired, lines to get into the city's lone merchandise store in Miramar where a simple sledge-hammer cost fifty-six dollars. At the nationalized health care clinics, the lines wrapped away for blocks: the somber aged, the ill, the expectant young mothers, all waiting, patiently enduring. As I said, they were not the source of the melancholy. They only illustrated it. No, the gloom seemed to seep out of the gutters and the pillared verandas and even the laurel-shaded boulevards. It was pervasive; a presence hanging over the city so tangible that it was always a little surprising to look up and see sunlight.

I drove carefully, dodging Russian-made Ladas, bicycles, and a few donkey carts. If nothing else, Cuba is a great place to drive a car. The macadam roads, if uncared for, are wide and fast. Soon, the traffic disappeared; the city blurred, thinned, and finally vanished behind me. In the next hours, I would see maybe two dozen other cars on that six-lane highway, most of them 1950-ish Chevys, though there were a few old Mercedes and one tired Ford, too. The Chevys were cheerful things to see, for they were brightly painted and their mirrors were decorated as if to celebrate a religious holiday. I always waved at their drivers as I passed, they always smiled and waved back.

On my trip in 1977, I had visited a few country places in Cuba, and I was eager to get into the country again. At that time in Cuba, as in Central America, it was accepted behavior to stop at a house and offer money in exchange for a meal. Though very poor, the people usually had beans and fresh fish or turtle meat to spare, and were glad for the cash and, perhaps, the company. In the early afternoon, I decided to find a village and see about lunch. The map showed that I was near Guines, a dot off the main highway, so I turned south and banged my way along five miles of sugarcane until I came to a settlement of houses on a dirt road. The settlement was dominated by a packing plant made of corrugated metal. Two soldiers stood by the closed gate at the factory entrance. I asked the soldiers about a place to eat. There was none, they said. Down the road, an old man sitting in the shade suggested I knock at the door of a building beside the factory. I knocked. The door cracked. The woman peering through told me she had no food. The door closed again.

I decided to try another village. Compared to Guines, San Nicolas was a metropolis. There were a few buildings of marble and coral rock. Judging from the rows of old houses and the sidewalk crowded with pedestrians, I guessed it was home to perhaps ten thousand souls. There was what seemed to be a restaurant: an open place of tile floors and crowded tables. I went to the counter, smiling at the people who gawked at me. No tourist buses came to San Nicolas. My car was an oddity; I was a curiosity. An old woman stood at my elbow, staring so intensely that she seemed to doubt that I was real. I ordered food and a cold beer . . . then wondered why the woman behind the counter reacted with embarrassment. For the first time, I noticed what was on the crowded tables of this crowded place—nothing.

"In the evening, we will have soup," the woman told me. "Only soup. But you must wait with the others."

The people outside weren't pedestrians, I realized. They were standing in line—and I had cut to the front.

I apologized, waved, and left. It would have been hugely presumptuous, cruel, in fact, to offer money for food when these people had to stand in line for hours just to get soup. I had a canteen of iodized water, and I had a car where I could sleep, if need be. I headed on toward the coast.

Cuba has an Everglades. I had to drive through burning sugarcane fields to get to the western boundary of it, but it was there. Beyond the village of Hector Molina, not far from the Caribbean Sea, the blackened miles of agro-industry ended abruptly, abutting a low-land dike and road where the sawgrass began.

It was a relief to be in sawgrass. Unlike the cane fields, the saw-grass wasn't ablaze. It moved like wheat in the wind, carrying the familiar odors of muck and fresh water and cypress. More than once I stopped just to get out and feel the wind. On a tree, I found a *Liguus* snail—a kind of tree snail common in the Florida 'Glades. It was yellow and white, beautifully banded. I watched four white wading birds, ibis, flush from the grass, and hoped to see egrets and herons as well. But there were none. The only other birds I saw were two black vultures cauldroning on high thermals. Nothing else.

Even so, it was good to be away from the sugarcane. At one point on my route, the flames had blazed so close that heat radi-ated through the car, and I had floored the accelerator in panic even though I was unable to see because of the smoke. I was al-ready dreading the trip back through those damn flames.

I had no idea of how great an area the sawgrass covered. The Zapata Peninsula, at one point, stretches more than sixty miles. In the far, far distance, I could see a rind of tree canopy, nothing more. Perhaps the best way to get to the interior of the swamp was to find a boat and explore up one of the mangrove creeks this Everglades must certainly feed.

I drove on south to the coastal village of Playa Calmito. It was a pretty place: whitewashed shacks with thatched roofs on a shoal-water bay. I parked the car, and a group of shy men materialized around me. I asked them about hiring one of the three small boats tied to the mangroves. No, it was impossible, they said. They did not have the authority and, besides, there was no fuel.

Who did have the authority? I wanted to know.

The men shrugged, clearly hoping I would not press it. I didn't. We stood around talking about fish and fishing. Yes, there had once been bonefish in the area, but no longer. There had been permit, too—but no longer. I didn't have to ask why. Stretching out from the shore were stop nets: fish traps hundred of yards long. After generations of this, the village had been reduced to eating salted shark meat that lay on tables nearby, drying in the sun.

I didn't spend a lot of time in the village. I had brought a bunch of Little League uniforms and baseball equipment to give to children along the way, but I decided to leave the whole box in Playa Calmito. While the women distributed the gear, I pulled out my map and asked one of the men about the size of the swamp his home bordered. As always, the map framed confusion—apparently nothing blurs the world like the imperatives of subsistence. "¿Quien sabe?" the man said finally. "Who knows?"

SCAVENGING ANGEL

On the drive southeast from the old conquistador city of Cartagena to the broad Magdalena River, my new friend Alvaro Sierra explained to me how he happened to get into the marine salvage business and why he was willing to brave guerrillas, kidnappers, cocaine *caballeros*, poisonous snakes, and God knows what else to probe Colombia's numerous ports and blackwater rivers in search of the rusting old behemoths he called "marimba ships." "I hunt for these derelict freighters," he told me as he steered his Mitsubishi four-by-four through the traffic-snarled outskirts of the city. "And when I find one, I buy it. Then I break it down. I cut out all the portholes, the helms, the lights, the ship's phones, the bells. On an old ship, you know, everything's brass, brass bright as gold once my workers sandblast all the paint off. Then we make these things into beautiful nautical furniture. It's my business. It's what I do."

Sierra stores his interesting quarry at a little compound set off from a narrow dirt road in an industrial park southeast of Cartagena. The place is practically a maritime museum. Name anything nautical—anything—and Alvaro has it stashed somewhere on his palm-shaded property. There are carved bowsprits and deck lanterns and teak booms. There are ship's binnacles and captain's tables and whole bridges taken off freighters. In a little lot beyond a stand of banana trees are big stacks of 80 mm shell casings from warships and a mountain of portholes. There are shortwave radios from World War II, cannon from Spanish wrecks, and an entire conning tower off a submarine.

It is from this briny junkyard that Sierra's small company, Co-Marca (Compañía Marítima del Caribe), produces its magnificent beds and bookshelves and porthole coffee tables. Sierra designs the furniture, his workmen build it, and they sell it a few pieces at a time at prices that would be considered steep for most Colombians but quite cheap by U.S. standards, especially considering that each piece is as solid and durable as the ship from which it came.

"It's my business," Sierra said, amending his former statement. "But it is also my love. Ever since I was a little boy, I have loved things that came from the sea." Sierra was wearing the standard uniform of the Colombian businessman: guayabera shirt and dark slacks. Soupy air rushed through his open truck window, and he steered nonchalantly with one hand draped over the wheel, freeing up his other hand for elaborate, tale-enhancing gestures.

Sierra is an excellent example of an ordinary Colombian because he is an extraordinary man. In a country so rich in mountains, rain forests, and seacoast, one doesn't expect to discover that its most compelling resource is its people.

Colombians? Hollywood's goofy caricature has superseded reality: swarthy little pock-faced geeks with Ricky Ricardo hair carrying automatic weapons and black attaché cases neatly stuffed with plastic bags of cocaine. Not that those swarthy little geeks don't exist. No doubt about it, Colombia can be an extremely dicey country, and few foreigners rally the *cojones* to tour the place. On the other hand, it's largely because of this that Colombia remains a thoroughly unpasteurized destination, which is one of the reasons it's among my favorite countries in the world.

Another reason is that Colombia is well stocked with fun, industrious Latinos—elegant people like Alvaro Sierra. "Something we've got to watch out for," Sierra told me, "are roadblocks. If we see something pulled out in the road to stop us—like giant logs, say, or maybe a couple of trucks—you hang on to your *pinga*, because I'm going to spin us around fast! It's embarrassing to admit this, but the roads of my country are not always safe to travel. I'm no coward, but those bastard kidnappers like to shoot."

I had to laugh. Not because I found the prospect of being shot amusing. No, it was just that nearly everything he said made me laugh, or at least smile. The reason was nonsensical but true: Sierra looks and carries himself almost exactly like Sonny Bono. Sierra has the same toothy, squinty-eyed grin, the same good-natured, all-embracing "I Got You Babe" style, plus a flair for storytelling that Bono and anyone else would love to have.

Listen to Sonny Bono warning you in a thick Spanish accent to prepare to grab your tallywhacker because guerrillas just might open fire at any time, you'd laugh, too. "I say this to you now," Sierra explained, "because it's always good to have a plan."

A plan? Never once on a visit to Colombia had I ever stooped to assembling a plan. It had never been necessary, because the people I met were so unfailingly generous with their time and so dependable in their love of adventure. It's a philosophy that suits Colombian sensibilities: Get out on the streets, out in the countryside, out on the water, and allow good luck and God to arrange the itinerary.

This trip was a fine example. I had arrived in Cartagena unannounced to old friends, without transportation and without a place to stay. Within an hour I was at a little cruiser's marina, Club Nautico, in the suburb of Manga, trading jokes and stories with

Norm Bennett, the Aussie expatriate who owns the place. Nope, Norm said, he had no rooms to rent, but he did have an old sailboat I could sleep on if I wanted. The boat was dirty, and it had no power or running water, but there was a shower beside the outdoor bar, and I was welcome to use that.

So for the better part of a week, Club Nautico was my home—and what a wonderful home it was. Each morning I awoke to the singsong wail of women selling fruit. They'd roam the docks in bright skirts, baskets on their heads, crying, "¡Mangoes! ¡Baaa-NANAS! ¡Piñas! ¡Aguacadoes y limoncitos!" It's a fine thing to sit in the cockpit of a sailboat and gaze out over the Bay of Cartagena while breakfasting on ripe fruit, fresh bread, and black, black Colombian coffee.

After that, the day was my own. Some mornings I would hang around the marina, talking to the Turk or Raymond the Irish Rummy. In the afternoons, I would set off on foot across the bridge into the old walled city of Cartagena. At night, I'd sit beneath the thatched roof of the Club Nautico bar, drinking Polar beer over ice and talking to whoever might wander in. This is how I met Norm's old friend Alvaro Sierra: he just washed up one night in need of a drink and an audience with whom he might share his finely spun stories.

Later, Norm took me aside and told me, "Alvaro's an amazing guy—a classic Colombian. No matter what kind of shitty hand he's been dealt, he always comes up smiling. But before you let him talk you into any half-assed search for marimba ships, get him to tell you how he got into the salvage business. It's not my story to tell—it's his." Which is how I ended up driving southeast out of Cartagena in Sierra's truck, absentmindedly watching the power poles and drab slums of gray plywood flash by, and then whole sections of agricultural country fringed by dense rain forest, listening to the man who looked and sounded exactly like Sonny Bono tell me what we were going to do if kidnappers tried to stop us.

Sierra was clearly avoiding my original question. So I asked it again: "Tell me, Alvaro—how did you get into the marine salvage business?"

"The salvage business?" Sierra replied. "I got into it for the reasons I said. I love ships, and I needed a way to make money."

That was no answer.

"I will show you," he added. "I will explain to you about the marimba ships, and then I will show you. That's the thing about you Yankees. You have no patience. Everything is rush, rush, rush. Be patient and you will see."

So I sat patiently and waited.

We were driving on a narrow macadam that passed through the little artisan villages of Arjona and Malagana and crossed a waterway called the Canal del Dique before carrying us into rolling foothills of equatorial greens and blues. We flew past grinning, barefoot children and wobbling oxcarts and a long, dolorous procession of Japanese clunkers with smoke-spluttering mufflers. Then we turned north past Barranca Nueva, where the air suddenly grew cooler—a little cooler, anyway—because we were driving along the Magdalena River, the main watercourse into the interior of northern Colombia. The Magdalena was wide and deep and stained black by jungle tannins.

It was through a clearing in the dense foliage along the river that I saw the rust-streaked superstructure of a freighter that had to weigh at least several hundred tons and draw more than twelve feet of water.

"That," said Sierra, "is what we call a marimba ship." Marimba, he explained, as in the xylophonelike Latin American musical instrument that's played with padded sticks. Because a marimba is commonly hauled out and played during village fiestas, the instrument is associated with happy occasions.

"Times of good harvests and wealth," Sierra said. "For the hill people and the very poorest people of Colombia, the late 1960s and early 1970s were a period of great excitement, a time that seemed to promise great wealth, because that is when these nasty, bearded hippies began arriving from the United States, telling us that if we planted the bags of seeds they gave us, and if we harvested the crop, they would pay us more money than we had ever dreamed of. And they did pay. Thousands of dollars. Tens of thousands of dollars. A million—money meant absolutely nothing to them. But can you imagine what all that money meant to a poor Colombian village? That is why those days were known as the Marimba Time, and the ships used to carry those crops are still known as marimba ships."

Sierra stared off into the jungle for a while and then said, "Everyone thought those were very happy days. But they weren't, not really. It was as if a deadly disease had come to this country. Many of the people who went to work for those hippies are now wrecked or dead—dead as the old ships they once used. That's what I do now. I hunt along the rivers and the harbors looking for abandoned marimba ships. When I buy one, I almost always buy it off a woman who has been widowed."

Was I still smiling as Sierra told this dark, sad tale? Yes, I was. I was charmed by his great gift as a raconteur, his love of creative profanity, his bawdy screw-the-world asides.

Besides, Sierra was happy now: he'd found another marimba ship that he might be able to purchase, cut to pieces, and reconstitute as beautiful furniture and nautical decorations—something constructive out of waste, art out of darkness.

Sierra hopped out of the truck and began neatly jotting figures in a notebook, making estimates of the ship's value. Yes, the portholes were intact. Yes, there were many brass lights. Why wouldn't he be happy?

After he'd made his assessments, we climbed back into the truck. He had a cooler of Polar beer in the back of his vehicle. We opened bottles and toasted—"To lost loves!" Then Sierra's monologue abruptly shifted directions, and he assumed a grave tone. "I should tell you," he said, "that I, too, was involved in the Marimba Time. Of course I was involved."

Alvaro Sierra was born in a Medellín slum in 1949. He ran away from home when he was thirteen, living a meager existence on the streets for a few years before deciding to join the Colombian navy in 1964. After eighteen months of service, he entered the merchant marine and spent the next several years working his way through the world's seaports. "A very good experience," Sierra said. "The only trouble I had was down in Darwin, Australia. One night, my shipmates took me out and got me very, very drunk and, when I awoke, I was still in Darwin and my ship wasn't. The *cabrones!* What kind of joke is that to play?"

Sierra had no money, no visa—nothing. To survive, he took a job hunting kangaroos (this was back in the days when ranchers considered kangaroos to be nothing but pests). "We'd spend two weeks at a time in the bush," Sierra said. "We were provided rifles and given five free rounds—after that, ammunition was subtracted from our pay. But I was a damn good shot. Some hunts, I'd make as much as sixteen hundred dollars."

Eventually Sierra decided to get an education. "I was accepted at the University of Toronto in 1969," he explained. "I worked hard. But then I was notified that I could no longer attend classes. Someone had checked my application and discovered that I'd purchased a false high school diploma for a thousand pesos. It had seemed like a bargain to me at the time—how else was I to get a university education?"

Back in Colombia, Sierra passed a high school equivalency test and studied anthropology at the Universidad de Antioquia. He occupied what little free time he had learning to fly a small plane—with an entrepreneurial eye toward capitalizing in some way on the burgeoning drug trade.

This was in the mid- and late 1970s, the freewheeling era before drug cartels and organized crime took control of Colombia's cocaine production, before narcoterrorists plunged much of the country into fear. For a man who had been running from the slums since the age of thirteen, it was a time of great temptation.

"I was arrested on my first solo flight to the United States," Sierra told me. "I flew from Cartagena north, and it was dark by the time I reached southern Florida. I was supposed to land at a little place near Miami—but all those damn lights! Who could tell where anything was? It was a terrible feeling. So I just flew around and around and around, and then I was out of fuel! I had to force land on this big, busy highway—441—at just after seven in the evening. I'll tell you what, land a private plane on a highway during Miami's rush hour, and you'll draw all sorts of attention. The DEA was waiting for me, blocking traffic when I got out of the plane."

You didn't try to run?

"Man," Sierra said, "it is very hard to run when you've got fifty kilos of cocaine strapped to your back. Trust my word on it! That night, I was on the Channel Five news in Miami—very famous. They had a TV blaring there in the jail, and when I saw myself on the screen, I thought, What a handsome bastard that fellow is! He could be a television star!"

Sierra spent five years in maximum-security prisons in Alabama and Florida. When he was released in 1987, he returned to Colombia without money or prospects. At thirty-eight, most people would have considered their lives ruined.

"Ruined?" Alvaro asked. "In what way was my life ruined?"

He was smiling—why was this man always smiling? "True," he admitted. "I had made a colossal mistake. I'd tried to get rich by doing something terribly destructive. But if I hadn't gotten caught, if I hadn't spent all those years in American prisons, I really do believe my circumstances would be very, very different now. Would I now have my beautiful wife and my wonderful children? Would I now be a respected businessman? No. My life would be as empty as one of these old shipwrecks. But I returned to my country with a great idea in my head. And this is why I enjoy what I do so much: I take the wreckage of the Marimba Time and make something beautiful out of it."

As Sierra spoke, his eyes seldom left the derelict freighter—a listing hulk slumbering in the black water. He was looking beneath the dirt and blistered paint. He was seeing gold.

BIKE COPS

News item: San Antonio, TX (Independent News Source)—On the final day of the Police on Bikes Conference, the obstacle course competition was delayed nearly half an hour while paramedics treated a Las Vegas policeman who crashed his bike after losing control in the loose gravel of an obstacle that participants called "Hell's Rock Quarry." Many of the 275 policemen in attendance watched solemnly as the Las Vegas officer was fitted with a neck brace and strapped to a backboard before being rushed to a local hospital where he was treated for shoulder injuries and released.

Implicated in a pending lawsuit resulting from the crash is *Outside* magazine columnist Randy Wayne White. White was in charge of raking the gravel pit between heats.

"White should have never been given that job," said one informed source. "Judging from the way he leaned on that rake, I suspect he's had trouble with the law before. Anyone who's watched a prison work crew will know exactly what I mean. For another thing, he was an independent entry in the competition. He had everything to gain and nothing to lose by futzing the gravel pit."

Contacted by telephone at his Florida home, White said, "San Antonio? I've never been to San Antonio. And don't ask me any questions about that damn bike contest, either."

Records at the San Antonio Hilton show that a man named Randy White was registered at the hotel during the dates of the International Police Mountain Bike Association's annual meeting. White listed his occupation as "Professional outdoorsman/Fishing guide."

Attorneys for the plaintiff could not be reached for comment.

Yes, so now the shysters are after me. "Could not be reached for comment" indeed—they were probably out waxing the steps of some Vegas retirement village, or perhaps mustering flunkies to track me down like a dog. Well, as every good fishing guide knows, you can't bleed white what you can't catch, so good luck to the Nevada ambulance chasers if they try to serve papers on someone in my line of work. I'd welcome the opportunity to introduce them to just one of the many Third World hellholes that are second home to me; places where *depose* has nothing to do with pretrial testimony, and *countersuit* is pidgin English for *coffin*. Say Sumatra: let their goons follow me into one of the alleys off Sri Rangan Street, then sit back and grin as the batak floozies peck them woozy. Or Borneo: slip some rare orangutan love musk into their laundry, then lead them off into the jungle. Nicaragua would be good, too: make tracks for Contra country and tell my buddy Captain Fuentes that, once again, the Commies are hot on my trail.

Oh, it would be fun to teach these contingency feeders a little bit about rain forest justice, but I doubt if they possess the grit that bush travel requires. Also, I'm not so sure it would be worth the effort. After all, what are we talking about here? True, I did attend the Police on Bikes Conference in San Antonio, Texas, where there was an obstacle course competition. True, I was an independent entry who, having nothing better to do, volunteered to rake that bastard gravel pit where the Las Vegas rider was injured. In all other respects, I am blameless—which is why I was a fool to even speak with the little man who sniffed around the accident scene and then ambushed me with sneaky questions. What was my name? What was my address? Instead of answering, I should have yanked the notebook from his hand and tossed it into the San Antonio River.

But I am a creature of habit, and it is not my habit to misbehave in plain view of 275 solemn-faced cops. And, after all, what harm was there in answering the little man's questions?

"Lawsuit," one of my new policeman friends told me, speaking with the charming succinctness that evolves from long shifts in a very tough profession. "What? Are you butt dumb or something?"

It was too bad about the cop from Vegas getting hurt, and too bad about the rumors of litigation that flew around afterward because, up until that time, the Fourth Annual Police on Bikes Conference had been a pleasantly informative week. Not exciting, mind you. Certainly not wild and crazy on the order of a hard-partying military-type bash, nor even as raffishly spirited as, say, rush week at a midwestern Bible college. It was low-key, quiet, and orderly— which, frankly, was a great disappointment to me. In previous years, the conference had been held, respectively, in Tucson, Las Vegas, and Fort Lauderdale, and I had heard rumors that fun times were had by all. Not that there was any whiff of scandal involved, nor any hint of churlish or even unprofessional behavior. No. But I had heard that some of the participants had relaxed between classes by racing their mountain bikes down ten or fifteen flights of hotel stairs. Or by filling the elevators with chairs and potted plants from the lobby. Or by participating in impromptu mountain bike drag races in the parking lot—innocent, harmless stuff that, to my way of thinking, is the kind of recreation that any kind of conference requires if it is not to be deadly dull.

But none of this went on at the San Antonio edition . . . not that I saw or heard about, anyway. Oh, there were a few faint echoes from previous years. One participant wore a T-shirt that read: COED NAKED MOUNTAIN BIKE POLICE, and I did witness one cop intentionally hose another cop at the bike washdown station—but he pretended as if it were an accident, and nothing much came of it.

Very faint echoes, indeed.

No, the Fourth Annual Police on Bikes Conference was, as I said, a pleasant, informative week. Cops, park rangers, and federal officers came from all around the country to improve their skills and techniques on what in America, at least, is an innovative law enforcement tool: the mountain bike. They listened to lectures on such topics as Campus Policing, Bike Maintenance, Tactics, Urban Drug Enforcement, and Firearms, then, in full uniform, pedaled their bikes out to the Hilton's parking garage for hands-on classes in basic and advanced bicycle technique.

In truth, this was all reassuring. These men and women obviously took their training as seriously as they took their jobs, and it is always heartening to watch people who are committed to what they do. After all, the conference itself was founded with serious intent.

"Bike cops came out of a mid-1980s movement to return to community policing," Donald Tighe of the League of American Bicyclists (the producers of the event) told me. "This conference is part of a national certifying skills program that provides a very specific and detailed sequence of training and testing for the use of bicycles in police work. From a legal standpoint, it is incredibly important that officers are certified because, if there's an accident of some kind, they could end up in court."

I would find out more about those possibilities later, but, during my first few days at the conference, I went blissfully and butt dumb from class to class. I learned about nutrition and fitness ("White flour and white sugar are killers!"). I was numbed by the weight of acronyms in the literature. (CMS—Congestion Management Systems; MPO—Metropolitan Planning Organization; ISTEA—Intermodal Surface Transportation Efficency Act.) I studied community biking, too ("The bicycle is not just a crime-fighting tool, it is a public relations tool!").

Dull stuff? You bet. But some of the classes were fun as well as instructional. In Sergeant Gary Gallinot's class on night operations, the Santa Monica, California, officer posed the question: "Where does a gang banger shoot a bike oinker? Just above the flashing red light." Describing a high-tech infrared video system for bike helmets, Gallinot said, "Toy time, ladies and gentlemen. Pitch dark, you can video the pursuit and the collar. Which is really bitchin'." Officer Stuart Bracken, of Tacoma, chaired a course on Urban Drug Enforcement that was good, too. He had these great surveillance videos of him and fellow bike officers swooping down on drug dealers, making arrest after arrest. "That's the great thing about a law enforcement on a bike, " he said. "The cop can see, smell, and hear everything, but the suspects don't hear us at all."

That's what amazed me most about the conference: the men and women I met weren't in the profession just because riding offered them a good way to stay in shape while on the job. They genuinely relished busting America's dirtbags from atop a mountain bike, and many of them had great stories to tell about weird, high-speed pursuits.

Bike officer Adam Kyle, who patrols year-round in Omaha ("Take my word for it—chain lubricant does freeze"), had some interesting tales. His first twenty-nine days on a bike, he made ninety-five arrests and charged suspects with 294 different crimes that ranged from drunk driving to possession of narcotics to garden-variety felonies. Once, he was hit head-on by a stolen vehicle, but Kyle remounted his damaged bike and ran the thief to ground. Another time, Kyle reached inside a car to take the keys from a drunk, but the drunk took off, crashing over Kyle's partner's bike in the process. "I was hanging out of the car, choking the guy with one hand, trying to get the keys with my other, and he was doing thirty, maybe forty miles an hour. I finally dropped off, but I wasn't hurt too badly, so I ran back, got on my bike, and took off after him." Kyle found the car and later identified the drunk. "A car can't take shortcuts," he told me. "An officer on a bike can."

It wasn't all work and no play at the conference. There was a bike raffle, a Mexican fiesta, plus the hotel had a small pool with a spa, and a sports lounge with a big-screen television. When the sun was still up, many of the officers could be found lounging around the pool. When the sun was down, just as many could be found pooling around the lounge. But the conference's premier events were saved for the final day, a Saturday. There was the World's Largest Law Enforcement Bicycle Ride-Along (WLLEBRA), a ten-mile bike ride from the Hilton to downtown San Antonio, with all 275 uniformed cops participating. And, of course, there was the Police on Bikes Competition (POBC), to be held at Hemisfair Park. I planned to participate in both, but the morning of the ride, an employee of the League of American Bicyclists informed me that he could not find a bike for me to use (which meant I was S-O-L).

This was a huge disappointment for a couple of reasons. For one thing, I hoped that riding ten miles through unfamiliar neighborhoods with a bunch of gung-ho cops would be interesting. As Sergeant Gallinot had counseled one of his classes, "There'll be thousands of people watching you, so don't go out there and act like dicks." For another thing, due to the flare-up of an old spinal injury (a bike accident, of all things) I had taken it easy during the actual riding classes, conserving my pain pills for the bigger events. Now it looked as if I wouldn't be able to participate at all.

So I drove to Hemisfair Park and stood around gawking as officials got the obstacle course ready. It was an evil-looking affair on approximately a quarter mile of tile sidewalk: twelve obstacles, including a balance beam, multiple curb jumps, steps, ramps, a boxed maze, and, of course, the gravel pit. I was chafing under the indignity of having to stand there as a dumb spectator when a kindly officer allowed as how it couldn't hurt for me to serve as part of the course crew.

Which is how I ended up at the gravel pit—a box ten feet long filled with railroad stone. The pit was unattended; so was the rake that lay nearby. When the first competitor went charging through, I picked up the rake, combed the pit level, tamped it, and stepped back just in time for the next rider to blur past. Rider after rider, I repeated the same ceremony. It wasn't demanding work, but it was interesting because I noticed that the gravel pit was the only obstacle on the course where riders didn't have to slow down. The maze, the ramps, the steps, and all the rest required caution, if not a complete stop. Not the gravel pit. Riders *should* have slowed for it. Railroad stone is treacherous stuff. But these riders were throwing caution to the wind, and more than one almost crashed before he or she made it through. (Adam Kyle was one of the few riders who had absolutely no trouble with it—and he went on to win the event.) Because most riders did have trouble, we began to call the obstacle Hell's Rock Quarry for good reason.

Luckily, I was joined at the site by a local police officer and an unattached rider, Mark, who had asked me to compete as a member of his team. (For a time, we were in third place—until my run.) These two men watched me rake and tamp after each rider. And they were still right there watching as I raked and tamped the pit flat just before the doomed Las Vegas cop came barreling through. The poor guy skidded out of control, then pitchpoled right over his handlebars onto the sidewalk. It was an ugly scene to witness. The Vegas cop was a big, powerful rider, and he hit the brick tiles shoulder first, landing with the resonance of a poleaxed beef. He made a shaky effort to stand, then collapsed again.

One good thing about crashing at a Police on Bikes Conference, there's no shortage of first-aid experts around. Within minutes, a throng of cops had the man's head stabilized and were applying ice to his wounds. A short time later, two ambulances and a fire truck arrived. The victim was braced, boarded, loaded, and transported in no time at all.

After the crowd-swell receded, I was left at the pit again, leaning on the rake and talking to my friends. Which is when the little guy with the notebook showed up, asking all kinds of devious questions, such as, "Have you had any previous pit-raking experience?" and "Do you have a beeper number?" He was the first to intimate that I might be among those slapped with a lawsuit: "It's being discussed. And you were one of the principals in charge."

Well, it's just like a shyster to confuse leadership ability with culpability. As it stands now, the producers of the conference aren't sure if the lawsuit will be filed or not. They are taking a wait-and-see attitude. I, on the other hand, am taking a go-and-hide attitude. By tomorrow morning, I will be two malaria pills away from this litigious country, and I hope they send their goons in pursuit—after the Police on Bikes Conference, I could use a little excitement. The poor bastards are out of their league, and unless they choose to hunt me on mountain bikes, they don't have a chance.

DR. PEPPER

Perfection is a goofball pursuit, one that's not only subjective but ultimately self-defeating: to find what you're looking for means the search has ended. Which is a shame, really, because roaming around looking for something is nearly always more fun than finding it. That's true of perfect waves and perfect country-side, and it's also true—God help me—of perfect hot sauce.

And yet I may have fouled my own premise here, because I think I've found a hot sauce that's uncomfortably close to perfection. I discovered it at its place of origin, a large, open-air building of tin and wood near the suburb of Mamonel, southeast of Cartagena, Colombia, on the road to San Jacinto, where out-of-work cartel guerrillas have lately turned their skills to the profitable business of kidnapping travelers or popping drivers in the head for quick cash.

But that comes later in the story. First you need to understand a few things about my interest in pepper plants and my search for the perfect hot sauce. In 1987, on my way to Australia, I spent a lit-tle time in Fiji. One day around noon, I put on running shoes and went for a jog through the steamy streets of Suva, the capital city.

Halfway through my run a tiny Indian man pulled his car off the road, hopped out, and called to me, "Sir—are you an

American?" The insinuation was obvious: only an American would be foolish enough to run at noon. I nodded that I was and then listened dumbly as the man approached me and, without offering the slightest introduction or briefest preamble, said, "Oh, thank God I've met you. I've just been married, and an American will know. Please tell me, sir, what can a man do to cure premature satisfaction?"

This poor man was convinced that his discomfiture was a symptom of being oversexed and that he was oversexed because of a cultural dependence on spicy food. Hot peppers, he told me, were well-known aphrodisiacs. He'd been eating them in one form or another since infancy: "It was in my mother's milk, I tell you!"

His family grew its own peppers—a variety of *Capsicum annuum* peppers, similar to jalapeños, that he called by his own name—Bombay something-or-anothers—and he was addicted to the things.

"I eat them all day, and it has warped my thinking," the man told me. "It is difficult to concentrate at my work. I can think of nothing but sex! I am like a machine!" He paused for a moment and then made a small amendment: "A very, very fast machine. It is driving me mad. I love my wife very much, and we are both desperate. Isn't there some pill that you use in America?"

No, I said, but it seemed to me he was ignoring the obvious solution. "Why don't you stop eating all those hot peppers?" I asked.

It was at that instant, standing beneath a shade tree along the streets of Suva, that for the first time I received the peculiar dopester's stare of what in these faddish times is known as a chilihead. It was a frenzied look, as if I'd yanked a feeding heron up by the neck and held it eye to eye.

"Give up hot food?" he said. "For what, a woman?"

Yes, he may have been a crazed and offensive man, but I humored him—and for a very practical reason: I wanted some of those family peppers. I later persuaded him to give me a couple of them to take back to the States. After I got home I planted the seeds in the garden behind my house just to see if they would grow.

They did. They were pretty plants, too, producing a banana-shaped fruit that turned green, then yellow, then red. Looking at those plants made me think of running in Fiji and of the troubled man with his new wife, and it also caused me to project the long path those seeds had traveled: all the way from some little village near Bombay, probably across the Indian Ocean, past Australia to the South Pacific, and then around the rest of the world to my garden on the west coast of Florida.

That was the beginning of my search for the perfect hot sauce and the perfect pepper. It was not a difficult thing to collect seeds as I traveled to the far reaches of the world, and whenever I returned from a trip I would plant them.

A couple of summers ago, I walked a pepper fancier through my little garden. He was an Alcoa-lipped brand of chilihead, which is to say that the hotter the peppers, the better he pretended to like them. He came to the little red chili *pequeños* I'd pilfered from a bush in the Bahamas. "These are nice," he said. "I've always liked these. Crush them up, they're good in beer." He was tossing the things down like M&Ms.

Then we came to the two short rows that contain what I now know are the *C. chinense* varieties. I keep them separate from the peppers I actually use, because they don't have much taste and they're way too hot. Among them were several chunky black peppers from Southeast Asia that I myself had never had the courage to try.

"You won't believe the heat in these peppers!" said the farmer from Jalapa, Mexico, possible birthplace of the jalapeño. "A wild and ancient heat that touches the soul!" The chilihead nonchalantly picked one of the black peppers and popped it into his mouth, and then his face began to change. It is said that the human eye does not convey emotion. Whoever said that hasn't watched a man recklessly eat a variety of *C. chinense.* The ocular lens cannot wrinkle, but it can bulge as if registering some hellish internal pressure, and that's exactly what I saw in the eyes of this chilihead.

"Mother of God!" he whispered when he could finally form words. "Man . . . that's good!"

I've never participated in these silly machismo ceremonies, which require the hot pepper eater to pretend he isn't in severe pain. Nor have I ever been interested in hot sauces that require users to dole out portions with an eyedropper. But collecting pepper seeds and bottles of hot sauce has become an obsessive hobby of mine. I've grown to like the way certain chilies taste and smell, and I'm deeply fascinated by their long and oddly convoluted history. I've come to greatly enjoy the slow glow that originates at the mouth and spreads north and south (which may be why some believe they're an aphrodisiac).

Now, whenever I'm cooking, or whenever I'm standing out in my garden, I can relive all kinds of trips: Cuba, Australia, Jamaica, Indonesia, Thailand, and lots of other places where people grow and use the little darlings—and that includes just about every region on earth.

A lesson in travel is what hot peppers are. Ask a schoolchild what Christopher Columbus discovered in 1492, and he or she will say the Americas. Ask a chilihead, and the response will be "capsicums."

Capsicum is a genus of waxy fruits—all containing the potent alkaloid capsaicin—that are indigenous to a large tropical swath of the New World ranging from Amazonia all the way to Mesoamerica. These plants were called *chil* by the Aztecs, and they have been on the move ever since. According to some archaeologists, the indigenous peoples of the New World have been cultivating and eating hot peppers for 6,500 years. When Columbus landed, capsicums were vital to the diet of many of the Native Americans he met. In a log from his second voyage, Columbus wrote of chilies that the "Caribs and Indians eat that fruit as we eat apples." In 1492 there were fewer than half a dozen species of *Capsicum* being cultivated in the Americas. In subsequent years, European explorers collected two principal species of peppers—C. *annuum* and C. *chinense*—from what is now the West Indies and Central and South America and steadily distributed them around the world.

Seeds from those original peppers probably followed the ancient trade routes, sailing from the Americas to Europe and Africa, on to India, China, and Thailand, where they were sold or traded by merchants who did not know they were revolutionizing the cuisines of the world for all time.

What was once a spice has nowadays become a way of life. There are hundreds of hot pepper societies around the world and hundreds of thousands of die-hard chiliheads who network on chili home pages on the World Wide Web. The present boom in the United States got started sometime back in the 1980s, and it's proven to be one of those exceedingly durable trends, like fly fishing and single-malt scotch, that won't let up. Not that I've paid much attention. My own interest in the subject continues to be random and solitary, though increasingly informed. Recently, for instance, I learned that my Indian friend in Fiji wasn't the first person to believe that hot peppers are aphrodisiacs. According to Jean Andrews's excellent book *Peppers: The Domesticated Capsicums* (University of Texas Press), this myth got started sometime in the late 1500s, when Father José de Acosta, a missionary, warned that their use "is prejudiciall to the health of young folkes, chiefly to the soule, for that it provokes to lust."

Chilies may be lust provoking (we chili eaters certainly hope so), but the missionary was sadly mistaken in calling them "prejudiciall to the health." We now know that one medium-size green chili pepper contains 130 percent of the recommended daily allowance of vitamin C—a higher concentration than citrus fruit. It's also known that capsicums can help prevent dangerous blood clots. There's increasing evidence that hot peppers can reduce inflammatory responses, including those in burns, some nerve disorders, and arthritis. Researchers at the National University of Singapore have even made claims that certain chilies can protect stomach cells against damage caused by alcohol and that they may also help prevent ulcers.

Not only that, but medical research has confirmed something dedicated chili eaters have known all along: that we, in fact, enjoy an emotional "high." The burning sensation caused by peppers triggers the manufacture of endorphins, the body's own painkillers. The euphoria is similar to that enjoyed by long-distance runners and other endurance athletes who have yet to learn that they could feel just as good by curling up with a cold six-pack and a couple of *habaneros*.

There is no country on earth, I have discovered, that is too poor to cultivate chilies, and there is no citizenry so downtrodden that it will not cheerfully discuss and exaggerate the merits of its own local stock.

In the mountain city of Jalapa, Mexico—where it is widely believed that jalapeños originated—I obtained from a local man a small bag of what he said were seeds from the "original and authentic" jalapeño plant that only his family now possessed.

"My family has treasured and protected these pepper plants for at least two hundred years," he told me. "Maybe more. You will not believe the heat in these peppers. It is a wild and ancient heat that touches the soul!"

Chilies may indeed touch the soul, but they contribute little to the intellect, as I once discovered during a trip to Vietnam. In the Central Highlands, I hired a car and driver to take me from Pleyku to Saigon. The Vietnamese are a great people, but their driving skills were handed down by a consortium of drunken French colonialists and former MiG fighter pilots, the net result being that the country's mountain roads are death traps.

My own driver was typical—a speed demon blithely unimpressed by the prospect of road carnage. Then I noticed a tiny bag of purplish black chilies on the seat beside me. I suddenly imagined that I had a kinship with this lead-footed man: we shared the same obsession. If I could turn our journey into a collegial hunt for pepper seeds, I thought, perhaps my driver would back off the accelerator just a little.

I let him know what I wanted. His reaction was enthusiastic. Yes, he knew just where I could find some seeds from an incredibly hot black Vietnamese pepper—and then he mashed the gas pedal to the floor.

I knew only a couple of useful phrases in Vietnamese (for instance, *Toi khong phai nguoi nga*—"I am not a Russian"), but I knew enough about the country's drivers to ask a Vietnamese-American friend back in Hanoi what to say when I wanted to go slower.

Now I spoke the word: "*Nhanh . . . Nhanh!*"

My driver chuckled and we skidded through the next curve, going just as fast as we could go.

I tried again, yelling, "*NHANH! NHANH!*"

No response. We flew over hills and through villages, scattering curly-tailed dogs and cyclists and idiotic chickens.

Getting the man to slow down was hopeless, so I finally crawled over the seat and lay on the floor, resigned to the inevitable crash.

Yet we didn't crash. We found some pepper seeds, we made it to Saigon, and it wasn't until days later that I learned that my evil friend—thinking it was funny—had intentionally given me the wrong word for "slow."

"You dolt," my friend explained, "*nhanh* means 'faster.' "

"Great joke," I told him. "Hey—try one of these black peppers. They're mild as Nebraska squash."

I've planted and grown many chilies over the years, but in my travels I've taste tested only several dozen of the hundreds of pepper sauces that are available around the world. Here are some hot sauces that I liked a lot, or at least that I found especially memorable: Red Extracto from Nicaragua; Majestica Hot Sauce from Singapore; Twin Elephants from Thailand; Tamarindo Pepper Sauce from Costa Rica; Congo Picante from Panama; Salsa Verde Picante from Cuba.

But recently, traveling through Colombia, I came across a local concoction that I believe was the best hot sauce I've ever tried. It was a pungent green, quite hot but not too hot. It had the fragrance of rich vinegar and crushed pepper blooms. It was simple. It was pure. Its name was Aji Amazona.

For me, successful travel requires serendipitous intersectings, and that's just what happened in Colombia. I was staying on the island of Manga, just off Cartagena, at a great little marina called Club Nautico. When I remarked upon the sauce, the marina's owner, an expatriate Aussie, replied, "Yeah—pretty good stuff, isn't it? I happen to know the guy who makes it."

Their little factory, Comexa, was a short taxi ride away from the marina, so I went to buy a case. I also met the proprietor, Jorge Araujo. "If you want to learn about peppers," Araujo told me, "I will show you."

Araujo took me out to the lush farming region where locals raised the chili peppers from which the hot sauce was made. As he drove, he remarked on the serious problems the area had been having with guerrilla kidnappers and bandits. Earlier that week, two German tourists had been robbed and murdered. I'd also heard that Colombian guerrillas were kidnapping as many as a thousand people a year, holding them for ransom.

Araujo said he knew nothing about this, though he did note that we weren't far from an area that "is not so safe." But all I saw were bright green fields and quiet villages and grinning children. Locals were selling buckets of wild honey, mangoes, and boxes of tamarind pods. Farmers were loading peppers, which would be packed with vinegar in tight wooden kegs and left to age for a year before processing.

Araujo told me that he had been in the wholesale pepper business, supplying produce to larger companies, when a "miracle" happened: an accidental cross-pollination. "In the fields," he said, "our growers had cayenne peppers, but they also had a local variety called *pipon,* a big, red, stomachy variety that no manufacturer really wanted."

The pepper that resulted from this fortuitous cross-pollination was a rare specimen indeed. "It had a wonderful smell to it and a very bright color like no other I'd ever seen," said Araujo. "We called it the Accidental Pepper. But what could we do with it? We decided to try to make our own sauces."

Eventually Jorge christened this accidental hybrid the "Amazona." Named for the region where all chilies probably originated, it now follows its pre-Columbian ancestors on newer trade routes.

"Have you tried it?" Jorge asked.

I'd sampled the sauce back in Cartagena, I said, but I hadn't yet taken a bite of the actual pepper. And truth be told, I wasn't sure I wanted to. For all I knew, it could be perfect.

THE MOSS MAN

I watched a white wolf kill a deer
Or was it a hot springs dream?
Don't know how long I've soaked here
But my hair's turning green. . . .

—"Ballad of the Moss Man"

The reason I was reluctant to participate in Ketchum, Idaho's bizarre and heretofore unpublicized Moss Man Commemoration and Pagan Fun Fest had less to do with my spiritual sensibilities than with the happy fact that I was billeting at the classic old Sun Valley Lodge, a mountain retreat of stone and wood that has captivated American legends since the 1930s—Gary Cooper and Ernest Hemingway among them—so what kind of nitwit would willingly leave?

"You can't spend even a day away from Sun Valley?" Ross Leventhal, titular high priest of the celebration, asked me. "We don't hand out these invitations to just anyone. There are socialites in this town—big-name *Hollywood* people—who'd jump at the chance to spend four or five hours up in the mountains, sitting in a natural hot spring, watching us perform the sacred ceremony.

How many nonreligious, nonsecular pagan rituals do you get a chance to attend?"

"Plenty. I'm from Florida," I answered. "Besides, the lodge *has* outdoor hot pools. A very nice way to spend an evening after a tough day of wingshooting or hiking. More importantly, I'd have to miss happy hour in the lounge. The bartenders here are very sensitive. They've come to count on me."

Leventhal is known locally as the Big Guy (he weighs almost as much as the massive Harley he sometimes rides), but he has the crafty, urbane social skills of someone half his size. "You oaf," he said, "I'm beginning to doubt you have the sensitivity to appreciate a celebration like this. We had a white robe already picked out for you— now I'm not even certain I want to tell you the Moss Man story."

But Leventhal, who lives a jet-setter's life yet claims to be "between jobs," went ahead and told me anyway. More than a dozen years ago, he said, a local man (we'll use the alias "Slim Becker") apparently experienced a debilitating spiritual aperture, which launched in him a desire for self-realization and the need to be "at one" with nature. "It is also possible," Leventhal said, "that Slim was eating amphetamines and had badly overserved himself." Becker, he said, hiked ten miles outside Ketchum to the secluded hot springs at Frenchman's Bend on the Warm Springs River and immersed himself in the ninety-plus-degree water. "At this juncture," Leventhal said, "details of the story are ambiguous and sometimes conflicting. It is generally agreed that Becker spent several hours in the spring before he realized that he'd gotten in with his clothes on. Who in their right mind would want to hike ten miles back to Ketchum in soggy jeans? So Becker did what should have been a reasonable thing: he removed his clothes and hung them up to dry. His instincts were right, but his timing was off. It was February, the coldest month of the year, so instead of drying, his clothes froze."

Becker, Leventhal said, spent the next twenty-eight days immersed in the hot spring, alone, without food, night after night, day after snowy day, communing with nature and, perhaps, waiting for spring to arrive so that his clothes would thaw and he could hike back to Ketchum in style.

"By the time some cross-country skiers found him and notified the sheriff's department," Leventhal said, "moss was growing all over the man. Do you understand the significance of that? *Moss*. He was turning green. Because of his patience and his dedication—and maybe because his pants were frozen—Becker had begun an amazing transformation. He was becoming part human, part plant. A lot of people talk about being 'at one' with nature, but Moss Man actually did it! Another thing that's interesting is that he reportedly had strange, American Indian–like visions. One afternoon he is said to have watched a wolf with pure white fur stalk and kill a deer—at a time when there were no wolves in Idaho. Can you appreciate all the symbolism involved here? A twenty-eight-day moon cycle in the warm womb of Mother Earth. A man who has turned green, nature's color of rebirth. A white wolf, a dead deer, a pair of frozen Levi's. It's all so . . . *symmetrical*. That's why some of us got together and decided to have a yearly celebration honoring Moss Man. We meet each November, the day after election day."

November? If they really wanted to honor Becker, why not meet in February?

"Because February's too damn cold," Leventhal explained patiently. "We respect Moss Man's accomplishments, but we're not slaves to his poor judgment. Besides, all the sacred beverages would freeze if we went out there in February."

Sacred beverages? I was suddenly interested.

"Yes," he said. "Cheap red wine because it adds a ceremonial flair that the event seems to require. And beer. Lots and lots of sacred beer. When one hikes through the mountains in a white robe wearing moss on one's head, then soaks for hours in a hot spring, constant rehydration is a medical imperative."

I told Leventhal, "Big Guy, you've got way, way too much free time on your hands. Next time you're inclined to start your own religion, my advice is you jump on your Harley and point that bike toward Baptist country. Those people can provide the counseling you badly need."

As it was, though, my attendance at the ritual was fated. "After all," I told him, "I'm a journalist. Studying the habits of people like you is part of my professional obligation. Not that I believe your Moss Man story for a moment. Twenty-eight days in a hot spring? In February? Pure fantasy."

"Drive to Hailey and check the sacred records," he replied.

"You mean the newspaper files?"

"Exactly. You'll find out I'm right."

I did. He was.

> News item: Hailey, ID *Wood River Journal* (30 Feb. 1984)—A 20-year old Hailey man was found soaking in a hot mineral pool at Frenchman's Bend last Saturday after having apparently lived there for several weeks. "Slim Becker" [alias supplied by me] was discovered Feb. 25 by two cross-country skiers according to a Blaine Co. Sheriff's Department report. The skiers observed that some of Becker's skin was peeling and that moss was growing on his back. The semiconscious victim was taken to Moritz Community Hospital according to the report. His clothes lay frozen on the ground nearby. A Moritz physician estimated that the victim may have lost sixty pounds while living in the pool. [According to Becker's sister-in-law] the man stood six two and weighed 210 pounds prior to leaving for Frenchman's Bend, and he took a lot of amphetamines. "His brains are really scrambled," she said.

Scrambled, indeed—not the facts of this strange story (the *Journal* is a respected weekly paper), but it *is* possible to present facts without revealing the barest morsel of truth.

That's what I decided after spending the morning in Hailey, going through archives, increasingly amazed by the Moss Man saga for a couple of reasons: (1) Becker apparently did survive an Idaho February alone in a hot spring; (2) Leventhal had, for once, told me the truth.

Yet I wasn't satisfied. How, in the space of twelve years, had the public perception of Becker been transformed from that of "a semiconscious victim" into a near-mythic spiritual exemplar? I walked down the street to the sheriff's department to try to learn more.

It was election day in Blaine County. The sky was autumn bright, the city hardwoods bare, and there were political posters in leaf-strewn yards. Although it was early afternoon, Sheriff Walt Femling already had a huge lead on his opponent, so he was cheerful and articulate and happy to talk. "I wasn't sheriff at that time," he told me, "but I was on the force and I remember the guy. It was winter and he'd been sleeping in the post office, and I had to kick him out. I felt bad about that. He seemed like a nice enough guy. Several weeks later, we got a report there was a man living in the water at Frenchman's Bend. When we pulled him out, he looked like a boiled chicken wing. He had moss growing on him. I remember him telling us that the reason he stayed in the spring was that his clothes got wet and he couldn't leave."

Other members of the department remembered the incident and added details: when Moss Man was taken to the hospital, he locked himself in the shower and refused to come out. "The guy really loved water," I was told. I was also told that Frenchman's Bend was no stranger to strange behavior. "Like the prominent local man who went out there with a bunch of buddies," one person said. "They were drinking and he got in the spring wearing nothing but his argyle socks. He was enjoying the water so much he refused to get out, so his buddies left him there all night—after taking his clothes. Which would have been fine if a church group hadn't shown up early the next morning for a baptism."

Informative as all this was, I still didn't have a handle on who the Moss Man had been, nor on what he'd become, so I spent the day trying to contact him. It wasn't easy. Both Ketchum and Hailey are recreational access towns and possess the fast-growing populace that such places attract. Many people I met were familiar with the Moss Man saga, but few even knew the man's real name let alone any details about him. As Leventhal told me, "See? It's easier to admire people we don't know." When I finally did speak with friends and relatives, they were understandably reticent about passing along information to a journalist. "He's moved to the Midwest," I was told. "He's started a new life." Finally, though, I was given his phone number, and on the eve of the Moss Man Commemoration and Pagan Fun Fest, I interviewed the man who has become legendary in the Sawtooth Mountains of Idaho.

"They've named a celebration after me?" he asked. "I don't know how to take that. Maybe it's neat; it's kind of surprising. One thing, though: I don't like the name Moss Man—it's embarrassing—but I'll talk about what happened as long as you don't use my real name. I've got a job now and people might get the wrong idea about me if they found out I'd lived in water for a while."

Thus the alias, Slim Becker.

"Truth of the matter is," Becker said, "I didn't stay in the hot spring just because my pants froze. I think what happened was, my *feet* froze when I was out walking barefoot in the snow. Like frostbite? It was February, I remember, and really cold and my feet got to hurting, so I decided to stay in the spring until they felt better. I guess I was kind of stubborn, but I wanted to walk out of the place under my own power. You know, like a matter of pride." The Moss Man added, "It's also possible that the drugs I was using had a little bit of influence. I was taking some speed at the time."

Even so, hunger became a problem. "I stayed in the pool for at least twenty-eight days without any food at all," he said. "At first I was hungry, then I just got weak. The worst thing, though, was being so thirsty. The water in the hot pool wasn't good to drink, and I about froze every time I walked down to the river, so I was mostly thirsty all the time. A couple of times, people came by on a snowmobile or on snowshoes and asked me if I was okay, did I need any help? But I refused because, like I said, I was stubborn. They didn't give me any food, but one of them gave me a beer. That was really refreshing. Probably the best beer I had in my life."

All in all, Becker told me, he considers those twenty-eight days a good experience. "It was hard at first, staying there all by myself. But after a couple of weeks, I just started feeling real peaceful. There were some great snowstorms and I'd just stretch out in the hot water and watch them. It's nice to watch a snowstorm in moonlight. Everything's so quiet. And wild deer would come up to me and sniff around."

Did he ever have a vision about a white wolf?

"I don't think it was a vision. I'm pretty sure I saw a big white dog drag down this deer. It happened right in front of me. At the time, I was so hungry I thought about climbing out and taking some of the meat. But I didn't. It was too cold."

The reason he accepted help from the cross-country skiers, Becker said, was that he knew he had no other choice. "By that time, I was so weak that I knew I'd die if I didn't leave. Not that I was scared. I wasn't. Like I said, I felt really at peace. I weighed two hundred and twenty-five pounds when I went to Frenchman's Bend. When they got me to the hospital, I weighed a hundred and forty-seven. The first thing I did was get in the shower. It felt so good, I didn't ever want to come out. It was a wilder time for me. It caused some embarrassment and raised some mental issues about me, but I'm mostly glad it happened. I learned a lot about the mountains."

Which could have been the words of a genuinely enlightened being ... but then Becker asked, "If they're having this festival, and they're basing it on what I did, don't you think I ought to get paid for it? If they're charging money, then I should get *something*—just for using the Moss Man name?"

As Sheriff Femling had said, Becker seemed like a genuinely nice guy. But, in asking the question, he also demonstrated that the Moss Man was human after all.

Yes, the man was human. I knew that better than most. So why was it, the afternoon following election day, I found myself marching in a column toward the mineral springs of Frenchman's Bend, wearing moss on my head and nothing but a swimsuit beneath a stolen white bedsheet that was spray painted with weird green symbols and the numeral "28"?

"You're not singing," Leventhal said after nudging me. "Why aren't you singing? Everyone else is singing."

They were, too—more people than I ever thought would endure such madness, all of them similarly dressed and, to the tune of "We Love You Beatles!," chanting, "We call him Moss Man / He was really keen / He stayed at Frenchman's Bend / Till he turned green."

"You take things too seriously," the Big Guy continued. "You insist on seeing this as a religious event when it's actually social. One of the things I've discovered is that people have a deep primal need to gather. Who cares what the reason is? Crazy people like to be with other crazy people—so relax, have a couple of sacred beverages, and make yourself at home."

"How can I relax with that cold wind blowing up my robe?" I replied. "I could be at Sun Valley right now where almost everyone wears pants. There's an ice show at the outdoor rink, and I think they're serving chicken wings at the bar."

"Believe me," he said, "you'll accomplish a lot more with us."

That seemed to be one more empty promise until I realized that a major objective of the Pagan Fun Fest was to march around the riverbank and the hot pools sacking the considerable litter left by previous bathers—an ingenious gambit that, as attendee Don Curtis said, "Actually makes cleaning the place up a lot of fun. No one makes a cent on this thing, and everyone has a hell of a good time."

Once I realized that, it *was* fun. I listened respectfully along with the others as Leventhal stood on a rock and read a poem in tribute to Moss Man ("O mystery of the mountains / I stand shit-faced before you once again!"). I cheered as loudly as anyone else when Leslie Benz, manager of the Baldy Base Camp Restaurant, was crowned queen of the Moss Man Commemoration. I too was moved by the speech of a humbled Galen Hanselman when he was named titular high priest for the coming year ("I command you all to continue passing the sacred beverage until someone sees the white wolf!"). But the thing I enjoyed most was when we all filed down into the hot pool—the place where Moss Man had spent his extraordinary twenty-eight days—immersed ourselves in the water, and meditated in silence on the fast river, on the Idaho snow peaks beyond.

"This place is so pretty," I told Leventhal, "and the Moss Man story is so weird, you probably could start your own church."

The Big Guy straightened his billowing robe and took the gallon wine jug from my hands before he answered. "There have been religions," he said, "founded on a lot less."

PROFESSIONAL WRESTLING CAMP

Because I expected to be gouged, GUT WRENCHED, or body slammed at any moment, I watched with interest as Rory Fox somersaulted over the ring ropes and landed spine first next to my chair. The resonance of bone impacting upon canvas stimulates primitive brain synapses, which is why I lifted my feet as if being attacked by snakes. Finally, I found voice: "Are you okay? That *had* to hurt!"

Fox's demeanor changed instantly. He smiled, stood easily, and vaulted back into the ring, saying, "Sure it hurt. Didn't you see my expression?"

Was he joking? Unlikely. He resembled an Opie clone from Mayberry, plus men from Watkins, Iowa (population 100), aren't known for idle banter. Yet, in the melodramatic world of professional wrestling, the only sure casualty is the veil between reality and illusion. But how could a spill like that *not* do damage? I'd come to professional wrestling school to gather insider information on exactly that, plus answers to other strange and esoteric questions. Was the blood real? How crazed did a grown man have to be to stand motionless while some goon thumped him on the head with a folding chair? Did all successful women wrestlers possess large breasts because of an evolutionary, selective function—carom devices, perhaps?

Stuff you don't learn on the sports page.

I had no trouble finding a list of instructional facilities. Big-time wrestling has become a mega-million-dollar business, which is why schools are popping up all around the country. Not so easy was choosing which of the schools to attend. Finally, I settled on Les Thatcher's Main Event Pro Wrestling Camp in Cincinnati because it is small and highly regarded by industry insiders. As was noted in a recent edition of *Wrestling Observer*, "Thatcher's students aren't even full-time pros, yet are more solid in the ring than a lot of wrestlers in the big three (wrestling production companies)."

Perfect. Staff members, apparently, were among the best at what they did. According to camp literature, I would learn "wrestling basics, aerial moves, personality and character development, and how to do television interviews." The "personality and character development" sold me. It implied an artistic, cerebral approach. I imagined the equivalent of a grappling boutique with noon breaks for healthy, high-fiber lunches, plus lots of emphasis on personal safety. Personal safety was a major consideration. Like many writers, I have a very low tolerance for pain—perhaps because we spend so much of our time empathizing.

Upon arrival in Cincinnati, however, I got my first lesson in the vagaries of wrestling reality. The Main Event training camp is located in an Evendale industrial park near Swifty's gas station, just down from a muffler shop and close enough to the railroad tracks to hear Norfolk & Southern diesels whistling their way across the Ohio River. It is one of fourteen rental spaces in a bunker of concrete blocks, consisting of an office and garage that has been upgraded by virtue of a wrestling ring and cushy spectator seats pilfered from someone's cargo van. On the walls are inspirational, hand-lettered signs, such as THE GIMMICK'S ONLY AS GOOD AS THE WRESTLER! and, BOY, CAN YOU MAKE FOLKS FEEL WHAT YOU FEEL INSIDE?

I liked the unashamed acknowledgment that theater, not sport, was being taught here. The place didn't have much to offer in the way of amenities, but that seemed unimportant to my nineteen classmates (two of whom were female). Something I soon learned was that, like actors, aspiring professional wrestlers willingly live spartan, low-budget lives just on the hope that they will one day make it to the big time. Like actors, very few do.

These people, ages nineteen to thirty-one, had come from across the country, paid $2,500 to spend six months with Thatcher, and were now practicing five days a week, holding down part-time jobs to survive. Several of them had been at the camp for two years or more, hoping for a contract from any one of the three major league venues, the World Wrestling Federation (WWF), World Championship Wrestling (WCW), or Extreme Championship Wrestling (ECW).

"We think about it every day," Astin Augustus Ambrose (Triple A), age twenty-two, told me. "It's what we live for."

Among the camp's veterans was twenty-four-year-old Matt Stryker, one of Thatcher's top prospects. Stryker, with a 1960s flat-top and the tough, dependable face of a farm-town linebacker, impressed me upon our first meeting. He was going over and over a short section of videotape in which, during a recent match, he'd done a back flip off the ropes, missed his landing spot, and accidentally knocked his "adversary" unconscious. He'd had to perform elbow-drops and kicks to his opponent's belly until the groggy man awakened sufficiently to pin Stryker as planned. *Your life is in your opponent's hands* is a pro wrestling maxim for good reason. One example: in October 1999, performing for the WWF, Daren Drozdov and his partner slipped while performing a "running power bomb," and Drozdov broke his spine in an accident that's left him a wheelchair paraplegic. In a business that competes for increasingly spectacular falls, serious injuries are becoming increasingly common.

"I feel like hell about my screwup," Stryker told me. "We're out there to make our opponents look good, not hurt them. I'm trying to figure out what I did wrong."

I found the man's reluctance to inflict pain reassuring, so I was pleased, indeed, when Stryker and "Surfer" Cody Hawk took it upon themselves to teach me the basics.

Not all of the wrestlers at Main Event seemed as good-natured, however. After my first day at the school, I was confronted by another of Thatcher's top prospects, Race Steele. Steele was a high school all-American football player and a successful no-holds-barred fighter before he made the switch to pro wrestling. At six three and 250, he is an intimidating presence.

"I hear we got a reporter in here," he told me in his Clint Eastwood whisper. "I don't like reporters. I don't like them at all."

Standing toe to toe with Steele, I said, "Reporters? Let me tell you something, pal . . . I couldn't agree more. Reporters are scum. But don't sell them short. They bite like horses and they know how to use their fingernails—or so I hear."

I would find out later that some fiend was planting anonymous notes in Steele's gym bag, one of which read, *Randy White is a former collegian champion wrestler and he's here to make us look like fools.*

All a complete fabrication. I can barely wrestle myself into clean pants in the morning. Was Steele serious?

In the world of professional wrestling, outsiders never know for sure. They call us "marks" for a reason.

"Don't rush!" Les Thatcher tells us. Twenty of us have him surrounded, a man to whom center stage is a vortex amid cables. "When you do a spot, take your time. Take the bump, then sell the pain. Remember: when you're in the ring, you're telling a story. So turn the pages slowly!"

By our second practice, I'd already assembled enough insider nomenclature to follow along. A "spot" is a particular throw or hold; a "bump" is the fall the recipient takes when he hits the canvas; the "Heel" is the bad guy; "Babyface" or "Baby" is the good guy. To "stiff" someone is to actually hurt them, to "juice" them is to make them bleed. Some of the terminology dates back to when promoters used code to telegraph scripts via Western Union to wrestlers working on the road. To "go over" was to win; to "go Broadway" was to fight to a draw; to "look at the light" was to lose.

Thatcher adds, "You're supposed to be creating an illusion, not just going through the mechanics! Every action calls for a reaction, and it's all got to make sense. If you can't communicate emotion, if you can't convince paying customers that you really are hurt or crazy pissed off, you've got no place in this industry. You might as well gather up your gear and leave."

Thatcher should know what it takes to make it in professional wrestling. He's been in the business since July 1960, when, at the age of nineteen, he debuted against Cowboy Ronnie at the Blue Hills, Maine, fairgrounds. He spent the next two decades as a wrestler on the independent circuit, doing more than three thousand matches at whistle-stop intervals, from L.A. to Indianola, from Charlotte to Manhattan to Moline. While wrestling, he also began to work as a color commentator, trainer, and promoter. He's been doing it ever since. In 1978 he was named Commentator of the Year by the Wrestling Fans International Association and, in 1994, was inducted into the Pro Wrestling Hall of Fame in Knoxville, Tennessee. Thatcher was never a huge name like Gorgeous George Wagner, but he was always a solid name and remains a solid advocate of the industry to this day.

His students trust him, that much is obvious. With his silver hair and precise goatee, he might be a very heavily muscled college professor. He leaves no doubt about who is in charge.

Practice starts (as they all do) with Thatcher leading "Hindu squats," a strange dancelike knee bend and a pro wrestling custom that he learned as a rookie and is now passing along to the new generation. Then he paired the wrestlers, experienced with less experienced, and called for six-by-sixes—a pinball exercise in which wrestlers carom off the ropes and either hurdle or throw one another. The choreography involved is complicated; intimidating, too, because of the constant noise—a rhythmic, rock band percussion of bodies being slammed to the mat.

Standing outside the ring, seeing things more clearly after only two days, I came to the realization that, if you don't have a gift for gymnastics, you probably won't survive wrestling school, let alone advance. The reason was obvious: reduced to distillate, professional wrestling is a very sophisticated and dangerous dance. There are hundreds of throws with spontaneous variations, all of which require athletic ability and muscle memory.

I have no great gifts, yet Stryker and Surfer continued to shepherd me and twenty-three-year-old Clint Copenhaver, another beginner, through the basics. First, we learned how to take a bump. They had us kneel at the ropes and throw ourselves backward, chins tucked, absorbing the impact with shoulders and upper back. I'd assumed that wrestling rings are equipped with thick padding and secret springs. Nope. On a steel frame, boards are laid as flooring, then covered with carpet and canvas. That's it. Land on your back from a squatting position, it hurts. Land on your back when you've been hip-tossed, it hurts more. Land on your back from an altitude six feet higher than the ring ropes (aerials are commonly done at the school) and it probably hurts a bunch, though I never had the courage to find out.

"I didn't think it'd be this painful," Copenhaver told me during a break. He was recently graduated from the University of Kentucky with a degree in education and a minor in theater, but decided to enroll at Main Event because it was something he'd always wanted to try. "I could have a job teaching right now, and that's probably exactly what I should be doing. But I've loved wrestling since I was a little kid. The way I see it, if I don't give it a try now, I know I'll regret it the rest of my life."

Intelligent, petite Veronica Stacy, eighteen, is another beginner and, like Copenhaver, fell in love with pro wrestling as a child. "I remember watching TV where these two big men were beating a smaller man, and I was furious! I remember thinking it was very unfair. Then in charged a nice-looking man and he rescued the guy getting beat and I thought he was wonderful." Stacy, who wears a two-piece camo wrestling tight and serves burgers at White Castle by day, added, "I remember thinking how nice it must be to rescue someone. To have the strength to beat off bad people. I've wanted to be a wrestler ever since."

Wrestling practice is every night but Friday. On the rare days they don't have to work, the veteran students—Race, Matt, Rory, Cody, Ben "The Bookie" Gerling, Neil Bzibziah, Jesse Guilmette, Taxi John Foley, Tim Moxley, and Dancin' Tony Bettendorf—do serious weight training. Mike Fergusson's Power Station Gym in Middletown is a favorite place: no frills, just lots of iron.

Race and I did a couple of kick-ass workouts at Power Station. Outside the ring, we socialized enough so that I've gotten used to the way he introduces me to strangers: "This is the dumb-ass writer I was tellin' you about."

What the wrestlers are all reluctant to do is meet for food or even a beer. As Matt Stryker, my self-appointed coach, would explain, "Among the major promoters, your physical appearance is just as important as your wrestling skills. We've got to look as good as we can every day. For three days around Christmas, I let myself eat what I want. Otherwise, I'm dieting. Who knows when the WWF will give you a serious look?"

I liked Stryker's intensity and came to trust his good-guy persona. More than once he's interceded when Race—outraged by yet another anonymous note slandering me—became too intense with his bullying. Surprisingly, though, Matt has decided to change his ring character from good guy to bad. "I'm tired of playing the Babyface," he explained. "You can have so much more fun when you're the Heel."

Wrestling is what the advanced students have committed their lives to. They live it, breathe it. Because practice starts at 6 P.M. sharp in the cramped facility, they all stand outside as long as possible talking about their profession. This evening, I listened to them discuss Vince McMahon, The Rock, and the dangers of "extreme wrestling" while a cresent moon rose over asphalt and corn stubble. In the far, far distance, Amtrak's sunset train to Cleveland or Chicago whistled once, twice, then faded into a muted, industrial rumble.

Unlike his students, Thatcher has no reason not to dine out or drink alcohol, yet he seldom does. Once a professional, always a professional, he says.

Yet he loves to sit over a coffee or Diet Coke and talk about the days when he was learning his craft, the days before the business changed into the circus it's become.

One afternoon at the Mongolian Buffet, I lured the man into a storytelling jag. "In 1960," he began, "when I was just starting out, pro wrestling was a closed shop. The few people in it protected the business. If someone walked up to a performer and asked if wrestling was fake, the standard reply was, 'Step outside and I'll show you.' And you'd better by God win that fight, or you were out of the business."

Did Thatcher ever have to step outside?

"Hell yes! A *few times* of times. We all did. That's why we seldom went into bars. Drunks are a pain in the ass and it didn't take me long to learn to avoid them."

It wasn't a matter of not being tough enough, Thatcher added.

"The willingness to take a beating was a requirement. My first week of training, the guys essentially just beat the shit out of me to see if I had heart. I kept coming back, but even then they didn't tell me it was all theater. They showed me the moves, telling me there was no sense hurting each other in practice. Save it for the match. Finally, one of the promoters took me aside and said, 'Okay, you're hired, so I'm going to give you the real story. But you tell a soul, you're history.' Protecting the business was always a primary objective."

Within the last decade, though, the secret has gone public. Perhaps because of that, or maybe despite it, television ratings are through the roof and associated income has exploded. There are pro wrestling products of every economic genus, including credit cards, action figures, and video games. Ted Turner bought what is now the WCW in 1991, and the WWF's Monday night RAW series is often the country's top-rated cable show. The networks formerly known as the Big Three are tripping over another to bid for broadcast rights to a form of entertainment they've historically rejected with contempt.

"I still get pissed off when people tell me they know pro wrestling's fake," Thatcher said. "Is a soap opera fake? Is a good movie fake? Yeah, the winner's predetermined in wrestling, but the throws are real, the falls are real, and during forty years in this business, I've never seen any fake blood, ever. It was always mine or my opponent's, or the blood of some other performer."

Thatcher paid his dues in other ways as well. "I got married a year after I started in the business, and it was doomed from the start. Same with my second marriage. It wasn't just being on the road and the groupies—pro wrestling has always had its share of those. I think what bothered my wives most was that they always came second. The business is my first love. That hasn't changed, and that's why I'll never get married again."

Here is something that shocked me: of all the aptitudes a pro wrestler must demonstrate consistently and without fail, the most important is the ability to memorize long passages of direction.

True.

At Thursday's practice (my fourth) Thatcher decided to test the memory of his students by "high spotting" an entire match, then listening while they repeated his directions. If they succeeded, he'd allow them into the ring to produce the same choreography onstage.

An abbreviated example of Thatcher's rapid-fire direction: "Power COLLAR and elbow, Babyface takes a headlock, Heel shoots him into the ropes. Baby hits him with a tackle; drop-down crossover, sets up for the back-drop. Leapfrog, stop, back slide . . . one . . . two . . . Heel kicks out. Baby works his way to his feet, headlock. Baby shoots the Heel off, takes a tackle; drop down, cross over, leapfrog, Japanese arm drag, cover . . . one . . . two . . . Heel kicks out. Baby sunset flips him REMOVE COVERS . . . one, two, three, match."

I was amazed that all the veteran students could *store this long dissertation away,* following this verbal direction without a problem.

Not me. Nor did I try. I had only one more day of practice doing throws and taking bumps to prepare for what I hoped would be my pro wrestling debut. Thatcher's best students work his Heartland Wrestling Association shows, an independent venue designed to give them real crowd exposure plus make a little money. Early on he told me that, if I learned quickly enough, he might come up with a spot for me to do on Saturday. Now, though, he wasn't so sure.

"When you take a bump," he said at the end of practice, "you sell it pretty good."

Damn right. There's nothing to sell when you feel genuine pain.

"Trouble is," he continued, "I take the shows seriously. I have to. If you get in there and it doesn't look real, you'll blow the whole illusion. I can't risk doing that to the other wrestlers. I'm sorry."

As he told me the bad news, Race Steele came up, gave me an unneccessary shove, and said, "You got a problem with what he's saying?" He added emphasis by slapping me on the chest hard enough to leave fingerprints.

"Damn it, that hurt!" I wasn't in the best of moods, and I'd had enough of his act, so I grabbed the former linebacker by his neck, vaulted him into the turnbuckle, then body slammed him. The sound of a bully flattened upon wood is a wonderful, retalitory sound.

But Steele wasn't done. He got to his feet, slapped me, cuffed me, threw me over his shoulder, and seemed to enjoy choking me into submission.

Writhing in pain, I opened my eyes to see Thatcher's smile of approval—yeah, maybe I *could* pull it off—as Steele (who'd secretly been playing Heel to my Babyface the whole time) winked. The last thing the big goon whispered to me before I "blacked out" was, "Hold your breath and blow. Your face'll turn red like I'm really choking you."

I'd passed the audition for Saturday's show.

"We take the show all over southwestern Ohio," Brady Laber told me, "but tonight's different because we're at the Eagles club in Blanchester. Cross the Blanchester city line, your IQ automatically drops twenty points. Scientists should use the place to study inbreeding. People with three fingers are considered potentially gifted. The Blanchester fans are scary, they really are."

Laber is the Main Event's business manager, but in the ring he goes by the name G. Q. Masters, a Heel manager, so perhaps he's trying to psych himself into character as we drive east through farm fields and winter elms. In the truck ahead of us is our dismantled ring, so there's a circus feeling, as if we are part of a carnival moving to a new town.

It is Laber who sometimes helps Thatcher come up with personas and stage names for students. The transformations are interesting; sometimes touching. Rory "Rapid Delivery" Fox's gimmick is to hand out newspapers because, as Steve Moss (his real name), he was once a paperboy back in Iowa. Dean Roll, who can't weigh much more than 160 pounds, wears a toothy mask and calls himself Shark Boy. His gimmick is to bite bad guys on the ass. Kerry White, who actually works *as a salesclerk,* plays the roll of Triple A, a spoiled rich kid. "Surfer" Cody Hawk's bio says he resides in Malibu and works at a tiki bar when, in fact, he lives near Dayton and works as a prep cook. Race Steele is actually what he seems to be—a straight-arrow ex–football star—but his real name is Craig Zellner, and he left his home in New Mexico with the full support of his family to make it in pro wrestling's big time. Matt Stryker is Bryon Woermann, and he works at a marina to pay for his dream.

These are the personalities Thatcher's wrestlers assume once in costume, but not before they've assembled the ring and set up folding chairs. As an audience of a couple hundred is seated, the performers wait in the Eagles club's smoky little kitchen, discussing final details with their "opponent." Everyone I ask says they're not nervous, but there is a preshow tension, and I, for one, am scared as hell. The village of Blanchester (population 4,206) really is home to some frightening-looking people.

The spot I've been assigned is simple. Triple A's ex-girlfriend will introduce me as a writer. I will say something derogatory about Triple A, after which he will beat me senseless and then beat his ex-girlfriend's partner senseless. Disappointed, the ex-girlfriend will knee her fallen partner in the *cojones,* then stalk off. Good, solid theater.

I pace nervously as Matt triumphs over Benny the Bookie, then as Cody Hawk revisits the classic surfer versus biker conflict by beating Bull Pain. It is a bloody strap-match battle that leaves Hawk with a split forehead (really) and dizzy for days afterward.

Thatcher is exactly right: some of the blows and all of the falls are real.

Finally, I'm on. I swing up into the ring and confront Triple A, who immediately flattens me with a fist to the head, then kicks me out of the ring. People help me up off the concrete and escort me into the kitchen where I surprise my mentor, Matt Stryker. Looking over his shoulder, I see he's in the midst of writing a note in a familiar hand: *Randy White hates pro wrestling and is out to make us look bad. . . .*

"You traitor!"

The man's smile is theatrical and evil. Due to turn Heel in a few weeks, the bastard's been practicing for the part all along.

It doesn't matter. I'm still aglow from my good fall and from the way the crowd gasped when bone impacted canvas, and also because of what a nice Blanchester lady said to me as I limped away: "Mister, it was awful the way he hit you! Didn't it hurt?"

I smiled when I told her, "Sure it hurt, lady. Didn't you see my expression?"

THE HORSE EATER, I PRESUME?

Having lived most of his life on Cat Island in the Bahamas, Pat Rohl spoke earnestly and with authority when he warned us that were we butt dumb enough to dive a lake called the Bad Blue Hole, then it was likely we would never be heard from again. "On this island, man," Rohl said, "no one goes about the Bad Blue Hole. Not even on a boat. You wise, you be doing the same."

Pat Rohl is known as the unofficial mayor of Arthur's Town, the principal city on Cat Island. This is probably because the little one-room restaurant he runs, The Cookie House, is the unofficial town hall for all public meetings. A stocky man with a wide smile, he serves up burgers, conch rolls, and local lore, speaking always in the pretty singsong dialect of the outer Bahamas. Which is why his warning came to my ears as, "Un dis iluns, mon, no un go 'bout de Bad Blue 'ole. Yah wise, yah be doin' dah some." We did in fact plan on free-diving the mangrove lake called the Bad Blue Hole, which is why we had driven up from Fernandez Bay to the north end of the island in search of information. The Cookie House seemed like a good place to start.

"Man," Rohl said, "the only way I'd go into that lake is in a diving bell, with a steel cable as thick as this." He touched his very broad forearm to illustrate. "That way, when the creature come to eat me, he couldn't bite through the cable. Them holes we got, they go deep into the earth. Who knows what lives down there? You never heard the stories about that lake?"

When we told Gaitor that we planned to dive the Bad Blue Hole, he grew silent. "That a bad place," he said. "Very bad. I would advise you gentlemen not to do that." We'd heard the stories, all right. Indeed, for the past several days, my friends and I had been traveling around the island, seeking out the dozen or so blue holes and collecting information about them. With me were Mark Keasler and his adopted brother, Andy Fox, both guides at the Fernandez Bay Village hotel, both Florida expatriates in their forties, and both hell-bent on discovering new ecotourism opportunities for their clientele. With his thick mustache and ponytail, Mark looked like a pirate—appropriate, since he had spent much of his life sailing around the Caribbean. Andy could still pass for the corporate manager he'd been until two years earlier, but the kicked-back rhythms of island living were beginning to show: he wore expensive slacks, for example, but nearly always went barefoot. Together Mark and Andy had decided that sure, the fishing and reef diving on Cat Island were great, but why not expand the options?

The island's blue holes—geological anomalies that are essentially deep limestone craters filled with clear azure water that connects to the ocean—seemed to have potential, largely because of the weird legends attached to nearly all of them. Cat Island, not to be confused with Cat Cay, a popular tourist destination near Bimini, has no flashy resorts, so it is among the least visited of the Bahamas and is still pristine in terms of scenery and culture. It's a big, brambled island with a population of only two thousand souls. Most of them are the descendants of slaves or British loyalists, and they take their traditions very seriously. Up until 1926 Cat

Island was known, both locally and officially, as San Salvador. Residents have always insisted, and most scholars today generally agree, that the island was the same San Salvador where Christopher Columbus first made landfall in 1492. But in 1926, the island's name was changed after the Bahamian parliament in Nassau voted to transfer the designation *San Salvador* to nearby Wattling's Island. Apparently, several influential members of parliament had received a gift of land on Wattling's Island and then brazenly hatched a scheme to drum up a tourist industry on the inaccurate impression that it was indeed Columbus's first anchorage. (They even went so far as to call their hotel The Columbus.) The name *Cat Island*, on the other hand, was an old sobriquet for San Salvador going back to the 1500s, when Spanish settlers imported large numbers of cats to control the island's teeming rat population.

Rohl wasn't kidding when he said that no one on the island would go anywhere near the Bad Blue Hole. As local writer Eris Moncur wrote in his 1996 book *Mystical Cat Island*, "Cat Island fishermen will readily launch a skiff or *bateau* and travel many miles offshore, but these same men cannot be coaxed with any amount of inducement to travel even fifty feet on one of the [island's] many lakes."

Not that my buddies and I believed the legends. We had proof that the blue holes could be safely dived. In our possession was a British Cave Research Association article that described a 1985 expedition whose members spent three weeks diving, measuring, and describing nearly all of the island's many holes. From our reading, we were confident that one of the underwater caves dived by the Brits was none other than the Bad Blue Hole. We carried a reprint of the article as we bounced along the dirt roads in Mark's dented Chevy pickup, interviewing people. We kept referring to the article, taking comfort from its clinical descriptions as we listened to the tales of horror—used it as a sort of psychological anchor that held us in the linear reality of the twentieth century.

Earlier in the day, we'd spoken to Gaitor Ishmel, an eighty-one-year-old authority on Cat Island lore. We found him walking home from his little truck farm in the bush. He wore a woven straw hat and mismatched shoes. He carried a burlap sack filled with cabbages and tomatoes over his shoulder. His skin seemed darker in contrast with the rock-and-cement cottages in the background, squat buildings painted bright yellow or blue. Even though he was stooped, Ishmel was a tall man, a man of great dignity. "You want to talk," he said, "I tell you about this place."

We asked him about the Bad Blue Hole. "You meaning the lake what's up by the bat cave?" he replied. "Yes, that a bad place. A very bad place. One time, long back—this about the Christmas holiday—a lady go to that lake to soak the sisal. The sisal plant what I still make my ropes from. This lady, she there by the lake, when she notice this big ridge in the water. Like a long wave I be talking about, and she notice this ridge coming in, and she run off screaming. Never actually seen nothing, understand, but we all knowed what it was.

"Not so long after that," Ishmel continued, "one of my father's horses died. So he dragged it down to the shore of that lake. A big animal die on this island, we always burn them or put them in the water. Me, I was a young man at the time, and I remember how it was. It was on a Sunday, and we pushed this horse into that lake, and in not so very long we see a big ridge in the water coming toward us, like a big ripple, understand. And this thing come from under the water and take that horse away. It drag the whole horse beneath the water. It vanish down there in the depths! That when I know a dangerous creature live in that lake, because a horse, it not a small thing, man. My grandmother, she told me the creature was a mermaid. What I know is, this whole island used to lie beneath the sea, and when it pleased God to raise some of it up to be dry land, it could be that huge creatures were left in them holes beneath the water. Giant octopuses, maybe—I don't know. But there something in that lake, man. That much I know, for I seen it my own self."

When Mark told him that we had plans to dive the lake, Gaitor Ishmel was silent for a time, distancing himself from us. Finally he said, "I would advise you gentlemen not to do that. It's a very dangerous thing to attack these blue holes. But if you *do* get in the water, what I say you should do is swim across it very quick, man, very quick and quiet. That way the creature, maybe he won't hear you. That what I advise."

Ishmel and Pat Rohl were not the only ones who offered warnings about the Bad Blue Hole. Nearly every person we spoke with around the north end of Cat Island was related to someone who had pushed a dead horse to the edge of the lake, only to have the horse dragged from shore. Not only that, but an island man and his dog had both disappeared on the lake while duck hunting, never to be seen again. We heard stories about the island's other blue holes, too: they were giant flush drains to the sea, one man told us, that would suck us down if we happened to catch the tides at the wrong time. Some contained a manateelike creature. A local girl had disappeared in one of the holes for more than a month, only to return pregnant, claiming that a merman had kidnapped her and was the father of her child. Mark, Andy, and I listened politely to these stories and then chuckled among ourselves. If the Bad Blue Hole contained an animal big enough to eat a horse or a man, the Brits surely would have encountered it. But they had already dived the lake without incident, and we had their expeditionary account to prove it: *Cave Science*, volume 13, number 2, August 1986.

Right?

The Bad Blue Hole is an inland lake of forty acres hedged entirely by mangrove thickets so dense that even on a bright Bahamian day the light seems to have been leached away by shadows and stillness. The lake lies off a sand trail called Dickies Road at the north end of the island and below a network of caves from which, each day at dusk, emerge thousands of fruit bats. En masse, the bats create smoky contrails over the mangroves, ascending charcoal strokes above a tree canopy of waxy green.

We drove to the lake, found a tiny cut in the mangroves—the only access point—and then waded single file through the bushes. We did it very quietly, just as Gaitor Ishmel had recommended, and looked out across the water.

"This doesn't look like any blue hole I've ever seen," Mark said. He was right about that. For one thing, the water was a turbid black, not blue at all. I had seen, fished, and snorkeled blue holes all over Central America and the Bahamas, and they were almost always small, abrupt bowls in the shallow ocean floor where the water was crystalline and the sea life abundant. This was true of the other holes on Cat Island as well. We had already canoed to one near Fernandez Bay, a place called the Boiling Hole, where big gray snappers peered at us from the gloom of caves. And we had driven to a couple of freshwater holes that were eerie in their own way but magnificent for swimming.

"This isn't a blue hole," Fox said. "It's a big damn mangrove lake."

Exactly. If there was a cave somewhere down in the lake, how had the Brits found it? The water was too black to see a crater even from a plane, let alone from shore. Puzzled, we returned to the truck and put on our masks, fins, and snorkels. We swam along the mangrove roots, spotting sergeant major tropicals and two large shad. We snorkeled forty yards from shore and found one spot that was twenty-five feet deep. I kept lifting my face from the water, searching the surface for the wake line that Ishmel had described: some large, dark presence vectoring toward me. I wasn't afraid of monsters, really; my worries were more reasonable and therefore more diabolical. I'd been to Lake Nicaragua, where landlocked bull sharks had devoured more than a few locals. Maybe, centuries ago, that same aggressive species of shark had somehow become trapped in the lake and survived by eating the occasional horse and God only knew what else. Or maybe the sharks could come and go freely through some hidden labyrinth of caves. I'd seen the giant saltwater crocodiles of northern Australia, where anyone foolish enough to go too near the shore is fair game. Maybe a giant American crocodile lived somewhere on the lake. There was certainly enough cover in the mangroves. As the British cavers themselves had stated in their report, "Until recently, certain marine and intertidal blue holes may have been frequented by seals, manatees, and crocodiles, [and] blue holes do . . . have the habit of producing peculiar species previously unknown to science."

We hauled out a little inflatable raft from the truck, and for the next two hours we paddled around the lake, using the anchor line to sound for the underwater cave that the English explorers had described in their report, an enormous dark rift chamber they'd called the Well at the Edge of the World. Mark was in the bow, doing the sounding. Over and over, he would drop the anchor and roughly guess the depth by the amount of line that played out. We tried one section of lake, then another. Rarely did we find more than twenty-five feet of water.

But then, at a place several hundred yards from the shoreline, Mark tossed the anchor and the line peeled out crazily, as if some monster fish were running with it. "Sixty feet!" he shouted when the anchor touched bottom. It abruptly grabbed and set, which seemed to indicate a rock bottom.

On my first dive, I followed the anchor line through the darkening gloom until I lost my nerve and surfaced. "Too murky," I told my buddies. "Too deep."

Andy didn't take my word for it. He went down and came up not so quickly, saying, "Hey—I think I got far enough to see some rock!"

I waited anxiously on the surface, eager to climb into the inflatable and get back to shore. Who were we to thumb our noses at a century of Cat Island legend? The creature—whatever it was—might be down there in its hole right now, seriously ticked off at having been awakened by the rude *thunk* of our anchor.

Then it was Mark's turn to dive, and we waited and waited for what seemed to be way too long for a man without tanks to be down there in all that blackness. Suddenly he came shooting to the surface, wide-eyed and gasping, yelling, "Our anchor landed right in the mouth of the cave! It's clear, man! You get down close to the bottom, the water turns crystal clear!"

I swam down through thirty feet of murk only to pass into a lucent world of bright greens and yellows, all of it domed in a huge bubble of clear salt water. And there was our anchor, sitting smack in the horse-size mouth of the cave. Not far away there was yet another, larger cavern. We didn't venture into the caves. Such an exploration would require serious gear and a lot more diving expertise than we possessed. But we had found the damn things. And the more we puzzled over the report in *Cave Science*, the more we realized that nothing in its description meshed with the size, the location, or the appearance of the lake. It seems idiotic now that we didn't immediately realize that there was an easy explanation for this: we'd simply misread the Brits' report. This was definitely not the Well at the Edge of the World. They'd never dived here.

Upon realizing this, we exercised the discoverer's right to name what we had found: one cave is now called Horse-Eating-Hole, in honor of the Cat Island legend. The second is Big John Cave, after Mark and Andy's late father. Back in Arthur's Town, Pat Rohl and everyone else we met were incredulous when we told them what we'd done and what we'd found. "That must mean the creature's gone!" Rohl said.

But eighty-one-year-old Gaitor Ishmel was not so easily convinced. "What it must mean," he said, "is that creature was down there sleepin'."

SWEAT LODGE

Even though it implies a spiritual linkage that I am reluctant to acknowledge, any explanation of why I attended a sweat lodge ceremony on a Yavapi Apache reservation, and of how I was chosen to play a role in the rescue of a sacred tribal Crow artifact, must begin a month or so before Christmas, in Sedona, Arizona—a town where America's lunatic fringe blends seamlessly with the town's loony center.

It was in Sedona that I found myself explaining to Pat the Story-Teller why a place that cheerfully embraces every form of goofball mysticism was, to a supremely pragmatic, clear-thinking visitor, more of a social oddity than a geographical mystery.

"You're talking about yourself," he said.

Yes—the pragmatic, clear-thinking visitor. Pat the Story-Teller recognized me for what I am: an insightful man.

"You're saying the town's too commercial?"

No, I was saying that the town was loaded with goofballs. But why be indelicate? I told him, "No, I'm saying that Sedona is unusual."

Few would argue.

Sedona is the hub of New Age Geomancy and Holistic Crystal Spiritualism. A thriving tourist industry has developed around the belief that the town lies on or near ten major "vortices," which are said to be the focal points of earth's electromagnetic energies. These vortices attract extraterrestrials who arrive via UFO to refuel on telluric energy, and also spacy terrestrials who come to spend hard cash at the New Age bookstores, the holistic health retreats, the retail crystal fitters and pyramid palaces.

Something else unusual about Sedona was that nearly every person I met was quick to tell me that he or she was part Indian. I met part Lakotas, part Apaches, part Hopis, nearly all of whom looked wholly like the descendants of Ward and June Cleaver, except for one—he looked Italian. That's one reason I was sitting with Pat the Story-Teller. Pat could have passed for Indian, he made his living telling Indigenous American stories, but he didn't hesitate to tell me that he wasn't Indian—a refreshing bit of honesty after a couple of days in Sedona.

"You're skeptical," Pat said.

I thought he was talking about the New Age Indians. "I'd sooner believe in Santa Claus," I told him.

"No," he said, "I mean you're skeptical of Sedona." The way he used the name, *Sedona,* assumed generic proportions—metaphysics, spirituality, faith, the "corona discharge effect" caused by veins of basalt running beneath old lava flows; every kind of desperate pretense and flimflammery contrived by man.

"You bet," I said. "But only because I'm so open-minded."

It was Pat the Story-Teller who suggested that I participate in a sweat lodge ceremony. I was reluctant. Though a professional adventurer by occupation, I am a tireless researcher by nature, so I had already paid for a "life reading" at a Spiritualists' Fair where I was told that I had been a medieval monk in a previous life, and that I now had seven guardian spirits looking after me, nearly twice the normal number—happy news, considering my lifestyle. I had also paid to listen to Swiss vocalists sing the microtonal music of extraterrestrials. All this after sitting for half an hour beneath a copper pyramid where, if nothing else, I was impressed by the way my thirst was sharpened.

I'd seen the ads for sweat lodge shows—a hundred to five hundred bucks per person. I was on an expense account; cash wasn't a consideration, but I was repelled by the notion of any further funding of Sedona's metaphysical money hole. I told Pat, "There's a sauna at my hotel. Plenty of seats, no waiting."

Pat said, "I'm not talking about a commercial sweat lodge. There's a man I know—I'll tell him about you. If he says it's okay, will you come?"

I asked how much it would cost. That caused Pat to wince. He said the only charge would be an offering of tobacco. I held up a can of Copenhagen snuff. "Will this be okay?" Pat winced again; his expression became pained. I doubted if Pat the Story-Teller would speak with the man.

He did.

The man's name was Dean Falls Down, a Montana Crow who lived with his wife in a Yavapi Apache housing project in the Verde Valley, more than an hour's drive from Sedona. I arrived just before sunset to find Dean and three or four local men standing behind a concrete block house tending a massive fire. Near the fire was a beehive-shaped hut covered with tarps. I approached feeling out of place, so ill at ease that I began to regret imposing— clearly, these were private people preparing for a private ceremony. But Dean, a wide-bodied man with onyx eyes, accepted my gift of tobacco gracefully, and he and the others made me feel welcome. Not that Dean said much. Not that anyone said much. We sat and watched the fire—there were logs in there the size of railroad ties—and, when the sun was gone, Dean said, "We'll begin now."

He dug glowing rocks—forty-four of them—from the fire pit and transferred them into the lodge. Then we stripped our clothes off and crawled into the lodge, moving counterclockwise on our knees beneath the low tarp ceiling. Dean was the last to enter. When he pulled the flap closed, the rocks provided an eerie, molten candescence: five gilded faces, disembodied by darkness, floated suspended in the weak light. Dean had a bucket of water and a dipper. He filled the dipper four times, poured each onto the rocks, and an astonishing heat filled that tiny place.

I didn't know it at the time, but this was the beginning of what Falls Down calls a "doctoring" sweat. This doctoring sweat was the result of an individual's request for spiritual help, and there were several distinctive elements—the most important of which, to a nonbeliever, was that it is the hottest of all the sweat lodges, and seems to go on forever.

But as I said, I didn't know that at the time; didn't know how to act, what to say, or what to expect. I sat cross-legged in my space, struggling to breathe, while the others participated. I will not relate what was said—it was private and personal. I will relate that, just before Dean spoke a final prayer and threw open the door, I felt as if there was a real possibility that I might faint. I didn't. I crawled with the others into the cool night and collapsed on my back beneath an Arizona starscape that was as bright as December snow. Dean sat nearby, smiling.

He said, "Pretty hot in there, huh?"

I answered, "I feel *weak* as an eggplant. No wonder they called your people redskins."

"The next few rounds, you'll get used to it."

I sat up. The next few rounds? Gad! Did he mean we had to go back in?

Dean meant exactly that. The second round was longer—and hotter. He poured seven dippers full of water onto the stones. For the withering third round, Dean poured ten. I didn't get used to the heat, but I did discover that, by hunkering down low, I could find little pockets of breathable air close to the floor. We had been given branches of sage to whip impurities from our skin. I began to lash myself with enthusiasm—anything to divert my attention from the sensation of being parboiled. The words of the other men also became a source of refuge—if they could find enough air to speak, certainly my own situation was not so desperate. I listened, I punished myself with the sage, I held on.

Prior to the fourth round, I had not spoken a word. How could I? But during our short break, Dean announced, "Randy will say the last prayer," which effectively torpedoed all the careful excuses I had devised for leaving early—"Sorry boys, I've got a date with a Swiss soprano in Sedona. Gotta run!"—and obligated me not only to endure the hottest of the four sweats, but also to find the strength to speak coherently at the end.

I would later learn that every element of the sweat lodge is symbolic, from the number of stones in the pit, to the direction of movement and flow of conversation, to the number of dippers poured. Dean began by saying that he would now pour four dippers—"Like the first round, because our prayers are endless"—but then invited every man in the lodge to request additional dippers. I wanted to ask if I could drink the water first, then transfer it to the rocks at my leisure. I didn't; nor did I request any additional dippers. But the others did. One man requested three, another five. I'm not sure what the final total was, but I remember thinking that Dean could have saved some time by just dumping on the whole bucket.

The heat was numbing. I flattened myself on the skin floor like roadkill, one hand over my mouth trying to filter out the steam. I marveled at the endurance of the other men—they were still able to speak! Their words reassured me in the way that canaries once reassured miners. Even so, my brain continued to tell me that I was suffocating. My lungs agreed. In a kind of delirium, I tracked the course of voices as they moved toward me around the lodge. Soon, it would be my turn. I had been taking tiny little bites of air, just enough to remain conscious. Experimentally, I took a deeper breath—and began to cough. I whacked my chest into submission with a sage branch. I have no recollection of how long the final sweat lasted; my sense of time, perhaps time itself, had been atomized by the heat. All that existed were words and darkness, and my own frail determination to speak a final prayer so as to end our mutual suffering.

It seemed as if a slow hour passed, and then there was silence—the other men, I realized, were awaiting my first words. I opened my mouth to speak . . . choked . . . tried to speak again, and, finally, a desperate sentence exited in a whispery rush: "God-bless-all-the-children-and-please-make-Dean-open-the-door."

It was not an eloquent speech, but it was heartfelt, and God granted half my request immediately—Dean opened the door.

I went charging out into the darkness and threw myself onto the ground. When I was able, I apologized to Dean for the brevity of my prayer. "I just couldn't take it anymore," I told him. "I was close to passing out."

Dean told me, "That's okay. Somebody had to say open the darn door."

My sweat lodge experience was not transcendent; nothing mystical about it—I believed—yet I viewed it then, and now, as gratifying beyond all expectation. Everything said within the lodge was touchingly honest and . . . human. Dean Falls Down and the other men involved were without pretense. They had problems, as we all do, and the sweat lodge provided a format of confidentiality in which those problems could be discussed. There was no hint of ponderous spirituality; no taint of starved egos—the catalyst of all that is sanctimonious. They were nice guys. I liked them. Afterward, we lay around, gulping water, talking and joking. I remember that we laughed a lot. Prior to leaving, we made the promise that all newly met people make—we'd stay in touch.

Surprisingly, Dean Falls Down did stay in touch. A couple of times a year, I'd pick up the phone to hear, "Hey, Randy, it's Dean," a greeting that, initially, caused me a confused few seconds as I tried to decipher who Dean was. Once, coincidentally, he called when I was struggling to decide what to do with some prehistoric Indian artifacts that had come into my possession. He offered advice, a portion of which seemed peculiar—"You need to wrap it in a red cloth"—but I followed his recommendations. Another time he called and, in the course of conversation, invited me to attend a Sun Dance he was having in Montana—four days without food or water, seeking visions.

"You're asking me to write about it?" I asked.

"No," he said, "I'm asking if you want to participate."

The offer was made so casually that he might have been asking me to go on a hike. I wanted to accept, but as a beverage-loving pragmatic, common sense won out. I declined. Even so, I wondered why he would offer to include me in what clearly was an important tribal ceremony.

Dean seemed as mystified by my question as I was by his invitation. "For the same reason you came to the sweat lodge," he said, as if the answer were obvious.

Slightly more than a year ago, Dean called again—this time, with a favor to ask. A thing had been taken from his tribe, he said, and he had reason to believe that it was in Florida, my home state.

"It's one of the Little People," he said, and went on to explain that the Little People lived in the Big Horn Mountains of Montana.

"You mean a statue of a little person?" I asked.

"No. They're people. My grandfather had one in his possession, but he passed it along to another family member and it disappeared. They're very rare and very powerful, these Little People."

My questions became more delicate—Dean was a believer; I didn't want to risk offending him. But to help, I needed to know what the thing looked like.

"It's hard to describe on the phone," Dean said. "It's made of flesh, but it might appear to be more like stone. It's about eighteen inches tall, with a face and a body, and it probably weighs twelve to fifteen pounds."

"Then it was made of stone," I suggested.

"No, no," Dean said. "It's human. But it might *appear* to be made of stone—sort of like a fossil. We're pretty sure that somebody in Florida has it. One thing, Randy—if you find it? Don't make eye contact with the Little Person, and don't have any conversations with it. That would be bad for you."

I asked when the Little Person had disappeared. He said, "Maybe thirty or forty years ago." I asked if he had any specific information about the Little Person's location. He didn't. I reminded Dean that a lot can happen in thirty or forty years, and that there were now thirteen million people living in Florida. Even so, I promised to find out what I could.

Over the next few weeks, I made a dozen or so calls. I spoke with archaeologists, I spoke with members of historical societies, I called several people rumored to be artifact collectors (though none would admit that they were). I did not mention Little People who lived in the Big Horn Mountains. Instead, I described a stone or clay statue that had once belonged to the Crow tribe. No one with whom I spoke admitted they had ever heard of such an artifact.

I wasn't surprised. With so little information, and so many years after the artifact's disappearance, no rational, clear-thinking person could expect to find what Dean wanted me to find. I telephoned Dean and gave him the bad news. Dean seemed surprised. "I felt like you were going to find it," he said.

Nearly six months had passed when, recently, I answered the phone to hear, "Hey, Randy, it's Dean." I thought he might be calling to wish me the compliments of the season—could picture him sitting in his little house, the sweat lodge out back, an hour's drive from Sedona where merchants were probably decorating their pyramids with tinsel and preparing to roast their holiday tofu. Dean said, "I'm calling to thank you."

I said, "Thank me? For what?"

Dean explained that one of the artifact collectors I'd contacted (he mentioned the man's name, and the town in which he lived) had telephoned Sonny Pretty on Top, the Crow tribe's director of cultural affairs, and offered to return the Little Person.

"I think the man got scared," Dean said. "The Little People are very powerful. I think this Little Person wanted his freedom. One of our medicine men met the man at the Denver airport, and now the Little Person is home again."

I began to ask questions: Dean was correct in saying that I had contacted the artifact hunter—but how did Dean know? I hadn't told him the names of the people I had questioned, nor had I mentioned Sonny Pretty on Top to the artifact collectors. Why had the collector called precisely the right person to make his generous offer?

This wasn't the first time that I had asked my friend Dean Falls Down, a Crow medicine man, to explain. His response was the same.

LAST FLIGHT OUT

It was Paloma Magallanes, a spirited but untraveled grand-mother, who unwittingly convinced me to spend a week in a tiny seaside village in Baja that I'd never heard of and certainly never planned to visit. I stayed only because the woman possessed a great gift that cast an ungodly spell on me. Fellow Third World sojourners will appreciate the reason: good food and lots of it.

Paloma is waitress, head cook, and owner of the tiny Restau-rante El Faro in Puerto Adolfo Lopez Mateos, a town of dusty streets, sleepy chickens, and wandering dogs on Baja's Pacific coast. El Faro is a pleasant open-air bistro with a dirt courtyard and six Formica-topped tables. There's a plywood ceiling and a bright seascape hand-painted on the front window. Off to one side, Paloma has arranged four old mismatched recliners, to facili-tate digestion.

Even with its few tables, El Faro's seating capacity seems opti-mistic when you consider the fact that the village of Puerto Adolfo Lopez Mateos has fewer than a hundred souls and isn't even shown on most maps. In a country weary of injustice, Mexico's ge-ographers perhaps decided it was unfair that a settlement so small should have a name that took up so much space and required so much labor.

To find Puerto Adolfo Lopez Mateos (whose name locals have efficiently shortened to "Lopez Mateos"), follow the Pacific coast of Baja south about three-fourths of the way down until the barrier island of Isla Magdalena swoops dramatically westward. The land shift is so abrupt that it's as if, in some long-gone geological epic, the island attempted to sneak away from its desert host but failed. Look inland and you'll see an estuary—Bahía Magdalena, or Mag Bay, as it's known to gringos. Lopez Mateos is to the north, where the barrier island squeezes close to the mainland. If you arrive by boat, you'll see the bare dunes of Isla Magdalena and then a large factory of blue and beige corrugated metal. The complex is fenced, and there are guards at the gate. This is the Mareden fish cannery, the village's only employer and one of two sources of income—the other being the tourists who come each spring to watch the annual migration of gray whales through Magdalena Bay. Lopez Mateos is, in short, a company town. Every morning, a steam whistle awakens the citizenry at six and calls employees to work at ten till seven. Ten hours later, the whistle sends the workers home again.

Late one morning my friend Galen Hanselman and I were walking east past the cannery, heading toward the white church at the center of town, when we stumbled into Paloma's restaurant. We'd been flying all over Baja in Galen's Cessna 182, and we'd originally just planned to make a pit stop here in Lopez Mateos—thinking, instead, that we'd spend the night a little farther south along the bay, in a place called San Carlos (an uninteresting tourist town, it turned out). But our plan began to cave in as soon as we sat at one of the little Formica tables. We could have sat anywhere—we were the only living creatures in the place except for a dog lying beside one of the chairs. Eventually, a chunky Mexican woman approached. She had a flat, handsome face with vaguely Gaelic features, and she walked with the swagger of a trail hand.

Had we come for a meal?

Yes, we told her, a light lunch perhaps. She nodded with the kind of approval that one associates with grandmothers who like to see people eat. We expected her to return with menus. Instead, she returned wiping ice from three bottles of Pacifico Clara beer and carrying a very large ceramic bowl. One of the bottles was for herself. She toasted: "To the good life!"

In the bowl was ceviche: chunks of raw fish, onions, varieties of peppers and tomatoes, all soaked in lime juice. Ceviche, made properly and served fresh, is one of the great concoctions of the world, the bouillabaisse of the tropics. But even in the best restaurants ceviche is usually a disappointment, if not downright dangerous.

Galen dipped a spoon into the bowl and tasted experimentally. He looked at me and dipped the spoon again. "Hey!" he said. He began to scoop the ceviche onto his plate. "You're not going to believe this stuff," he said. "It's really good."

No, it was great. Maybe the best ceviche I'd ever had. Next Paloma brought salad, tortillas, and a bowl of frijoles. "My God," Galen said. "These beans! Have you tried the beans?"

Keep in mind that we'd been flying all over Baja, a great peninsula in a great nation where people really know how to make beans. But truly, Paloma's beans were the beans of an artist.

Then she brought out a platter of grilled fish. It was corvina, a genus common in coastal Mexico and closely related to the weakfish of the Atlantic seaboard. It's a nice fish to eat, very mild tasting, but not particularly firm. Yet somehow Paloma's artistry transcended the frailties of the species.

Galen and I sat there feasting, and Paloma kept bringing food. We hadn't ordered; there were no menus. But we'd come for a meal, and that's what the woman was serving us. As we ate, she'd sometimes swing into a chair at our table and talk. Had we come in the small plane that recently landed? Yes, we'd come in the small plane—which seemed to either interest her or impress her, I couldn't tell which. Did we like the food? Yes, we loved the food—which made her grin. We were very lucky to have this fish, she said. It was the last she had. "I buy only fresh fish!" she said. "The fishermen know that I'm very fussy!"

As we ate dessert (papaya with lime juice and sliced wild oranges), I noticed Galen glancing at his watch. "I guess we have to get going, huh?" I said.

"Yeah, I guess so," he said. He was drumming his fingers on the table. "But, my God, that was really some meal."

"The best."

"Extraordinary."

"Really extraordinary."

I wondered if Galen was contemplating the same thing I was. "When you think about it," I said, "discovering great food on the road, food this good, is a rare thing indeed." He was nodding his head. "Can you imagine what it would be like to eat dinner here?"

You bet I could imagine it. Dinner, breakfast, too, and maybe lunch again. The only problem was, Paloma really was out of fish.

No problem. On Hanselman's plane I had stowed a fifteen-horsepower Mercury outboard motor and a beautiful little Avon inflatable boat. And as I've already explained, the village of Puerto Adolfo Lopez Mateos is on Magdalena Bay, a place teeming with fish.

Bahía Magdalena is formed by a 130-mile-long string of sand barrier islands that are separated by deep-water cuts or passes (*bocas*, they are called), which allow ingress from the Pacific and which have made the bay a favorite harbor on this isolated coast. Its history is not unlike the history of all wild anchorages that are rich in resources except for one: fresh water. Although indigenous people lived here off and on since before the time of Christ, they were necessarily migratory. In the late 1800s, a U.S. land company settled five thousand Americans on the bay, but the colony failed. It wasn't until the late 1930s, when deep wells were sunk, that the region slowly began to acquire a permanent populace.

Mag Bay's backwater littoral remains pristine, wind cropped, wild with light, and seldom traveled. There's a good reason for this: it's extremely shallow, sometimes just a couple of feet deep, a fact that poses serious access problems and makes it a perfect place for sea kayaks and fast little inflatables like the Avon.

I tried to explain all this to Galen; the man is brilliant when it comes to aviation, but he's from Idaho, for God's sake, and knows nothing about the sea. I told him, "Visit any of the remote estuaries in the world, and the problem is always access. It's frustrating. All the fish you could ever want to catch, great birding and exploring, but you can't get on the water. This little Avon changes all that. We can go anyplace."

Galen was dubious. All week long, the wind had blown a steady twenty knots but on this cloudy afternoon had freshened to twenty-five. The bay had a menacing arctic glow about it. Still, we were headed for the mangrove estuaries, not the open sea. And we were prepared. We'd packed several gallons of water, flashlights, military-issue MREs, and paddles. Besides, we were on a mission: The Restaurante El Faro needed fish. We weren't just fishermen; we were providers. True, we mostly wanted to provide for ourselves, but the mandate was compelling even if the intent was selfish. Anglers and travelers must be allowed our small dishonesties.

I indulged in a second dishonesty. I'd read here and there that one of my favorite gamefish, the snook, also known as robalo, could possibly be caught in Magdalena Bay. None of the writers, however, claimed to have caught one, nor did they claim to know anyone who had. Indeed, the tone of the articles treated the snook like a shadowy creature of Baja legend. Well I, for one, wanted to prove that snook could indeed be caught in Mag Bay.

That afternoon we headed out in the Avon, crashing through waves. We went north along the mainland shore until I found a mangrove point where there was an interesting confluence of tidal rips. It looked like a good place to fish.

My first cast—boom. I played and landed a big corvina. Second cast—boom. I played and landed a California halibut that had to weigh ten pounds. A few casts later, I got a nice sea bass.

Galen didn't try to hide his surprise. "You actually caught something!" He hustled toward the boat to get his rod.

Back in the village, Galen and I drew a crowd as we walked through the streets shouldering the weight of a stringer full of fish. In the evening, lounging in one of the big mismatched recliners after one of the finest dinners I've ever had, I said to Galen, "You know, we can leave tomorrow, but I'd bet anything there are snook on that point. I'd hate to fly out without proving it." I proceeded to give a detailed explanation of tides and habitat to prove that my claim had merit.

He not only accepted this fiction; he embraced it. "Snook, damn right," he said. "They've got to be there. We should stay."

We did. For several days. We ate, we fished, we slept, and then we ate and fished some more—though we never saw a single snook. In the evenings, Galen and I would roam the streets, listening to the music emanating from the white church, conversing with the local fishermen at the docks. They claimed they often caught robalo. We never saw one among the piles of fish they did catch, but they were good stories to hear as we stood among the mud and small boats, drinking beer with them.

We'd rented a cheap room at a boardinghouse, but the restaurant was our real home. We stopped there three or four times a day. At each meal, Paloma, brilliant Paloma, who had achieved an expanded artistry in this small, small place, swaggered about, bringing us more of this, more of that. She spent more and more time sitting at our table, asking us about places we'd been, places we were going, and she seemed particularly interested in Galen's Cessna. "Many men in this village would be afraid to leave the ground in a plane," she boasted. "But not me! I would never be afraid!"

It finally dawned on us. "She wants to go for a ride," Galen said.

So on our last morning in Puerto Adolfo Lopez Mateos, we escorted Paloma Magallanes of the Restaurante El Faro through dusty streets to the landing strip. It was early. The steam whistle had just called villagers to work at the Mareden cannery, but Paloma ignored their stares with a regal indifference.

It was no wonder that they stared. Despite the intense morning heat, Paloma wore a long dress, a cape, jewelry, makeup, and a furry hat that came down over her ears. Also, the sand apparently made it difficult to walk in high heels.

When I told her that she looked as if she were going to a party, this normally talkative woman didn't reply. Indeed, she said nothing until we were banking over the emptiness of Magdalena Bay. It was then that she finally braved her first peek out the window, touched her face with trembling fingers, and smiled.

There was no swagger in her smile, only a trace of wistfulness. For the first time, she looked down on the little swatch of bleached sand and turquoise sea that had defined her entire life. "It's something I always wanted to do," she said. "I always wanted to know what it feels like, just once, to fly away."